DATA
PROCESSING

Data Processing seeks to provide an introduction and an
effective guide to the uses of computers in business. In
chapter 1, the author discusses the computer and those features of it relevant to business use, also programming details.
In chapters 2 to 4 computer applications common to every
type of business (for example, in Payrolling, Stores/Account-
ing, Production/Distribution) are examined. Further computer applications, for particular types of enterprise (such as
banking, insurance, local government and transport), are
dealt with in chapters 5 to 9. Finally, the author discusses
some advanced computer-based techniques relevant to company planning.

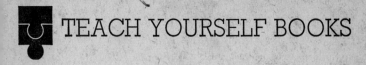
TEACH YOURSELF BOOKS

DATA
PROCESSING

K. N. Dodd

ST PAUL'S HOUSE WARWICK LANE LONDON EC4P 4AH

First printed 1969
Second impression 1974

ISBN 0 340 05398 4

Printed and bound in Great Britain for The English Universities
Press Ltd by Butler & Tanner Ltd, Frome and London

Contents

Introduction

Nine out of every ten computers at present being manufactured are for applications in business. In the period 1965–70, we are witnessing a substantial increase in business computing in Britain. The 2000 computers in operation in 1967 will have been doubled by the end of the decade, after which there will be a further, if slower, increase.

A computer has the ability to store information, to perform arithmetic and to take elementary decisions. This combination has enabled computers to find a very wide range of applications, far wider than for any previous type of machinery. The electronic digital computer, having these abilities, has been in existence since 1946. It has taken twenty years, however, for the computer to be perfected to the level necessary for general business use. Reliability of operation is obviously an essential requirement and computer reliability has greatly improved with the advent of transistor electronics. Speed of operation is not as essential in business as in some scientific and military applications but computer cost is a vital factor and research is continuing with a view to steadily reducing it. Indeed, we are now at the point where a computer can perform a variety of business tasks at lower cost than by using human labour. This means that companies can consider installing a computer as an economic proposition in spite of the heavy capital outlay. Thus it is that there is such a great expansion in computer sales at the present time.

In the United States the introduction of computers occurred some years earlier than in Britain. It should not be concluded from this that Britain is 'behind' in the computer field. The explanation is that owing to the higher cost of clerical labour in America, computers were able to compete in the business world at an earlier stage of their development than has been possible in Britain. As yet, only the largest firms are using computers here. Of the small to medium sized firms employing a few hundred persons, only one per cent are using computers. This indicates the potential for future expansion in the computer field. British industry will move forward in this field as and when the computer appears to offer advantages over traditional methods.

A computer is a machine and as such it has many similarities with other machines. In particular, it requires human labour to create it and to maintain it in working order. Most machines are made to perform particular tasks in a process of production and improvements in one type of machine do not affect other types of production. The great difference in the case of the computer is that it can be used in aspects of business which are common to all companies, namely, in the office work and administration. Thus, any improvement in computers will affect all companies, no matter what their purpose is. This is why the introduction of computers is called the Computer Revolution.

In view of this ability of the computer to displace labour particularly in clerical work, it is natural to ask if the Computer Revolution will produce considerable amounts of unemployment. In Britain this is unlikely to be the case for three reasons. In the first place, clerical work is performed to a considerable extent by temporary female labour. The intake of such labour can be reduced instead of declaring existing staff redundant. Secondly, many of the companies which are installing computers are expanding, so clerical workers displaced by the computer can usually be employed on other types of work. Finally, the computer itself will give rise to a number of jobs for which clerks can be trained. On the basis of experience so far, it may be stated that in Britain, computers have had a negligible effect on employment compared with variations in world trade and difficulties arising from the country's overseas balance of payments. In the United States, where labour costs are higher, computers have had a more powerful effect and have caused significant unemployment. In Eastern countries, computers have made little impact owing to the cheapness of human labour.

Apart from the question of unemployment, the Computer Revolution will significantly affect the structure of all large business concerns. We have already mentioned the application of computers to routine office work but when fully utilized they will also be able to handle many tasks now undertaken by management. This is affecting the types of position in the management hierarchy and all members of the management team must increasingly appreciate the activities of the company's computer. The overall aim of the computer in business must be to improve the efficiency of a company by giving the management a more detailed and up-to-date picture of the company's activities in addition to providing the most effective means of dealing with all routine clerical work. This aim for an *integrated system* is not yet achieved by many present day computer installations and we may have to wait until the next decade to see just how computers can be most effectively used in the differing types of business organization.

Our subject is already a vast and fast-growing one, which cannot be covered in detail in a book of this size.

It is thus necessary for us to limit our consideration to those applications of the computer which are finding the widest use in the business field. In Chapter 1, we shall introduce the computer and those features of it which we shall need for our study, but programming details can be omitted at a first reading. In the next three chapters we shall consider computer applications which are common to almost every type of business, then in Chapters 5 to 9 we shall consider computer applications for particular types of company. Finally, we shall look at some of the advanced techniques which are helpful in company planning. Our approach will be to explain the processes which the computer undertakes and how these fit in with the working of the rest of the organization. It will thus be necessary to describe the activities of the business world, in as much as they relate to our subject. In view of the complexity of some of the applications, our account will necessarily involve some simplification for the sake of clarity.

We shall limit our subject by excluding the application of computers and electronic techniques to the actual processes of manufacture. We shall also exclude the many technical and scientific purposes to which computers are being applied in industry.

In the preparation of this book, the author has visited a number of computer installations and he wishes to express his thanks to the British firms and organizations mentioned in the text for readily providing information.

It is hoped that the book will be of interest to students in commercial courses at all levels, as well as to the general reader.

1 The Modern Computer

As was mentioned in the Introduction, a computer has the ability to store information, to perform arithmetic and to take elementary decisions. Before considering these activities in more detail, it will be instructive to see how arithmetic can be performed on the computer's predecessor, namely the desk calculator.

Desk Calculator

The basic processes of arithmetic are addition (+), subtraction (−), multiplication (×) and division (÷). A simple electric desk calculator for performing these operations might have arrangements for holding two

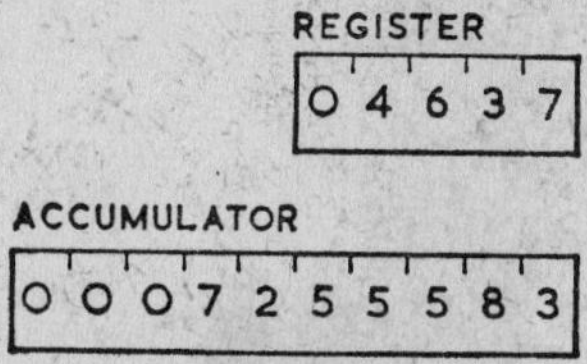

REGISTER

0	4	6	3	7

ACCUMULATOR

0	0	0	7	2	5	5	5	8	3

Fig. 1.1

numbers as indicated in Fig. 1.1. Here the rectangles represent the *registers* holding the numbers and the numbers show up on the machine due to the rotation of wheels on which the numbers are painted. Fig. 1.1 shows a five-figure register and a ten-figure one called the *accumulator*. Our calculator has on it a set of buttons marked from 0 to 9 and by pressing these appropriately, any desired five-figure number can be made to show up in the register. This is the method by which numerical information is supplied to the machine. The type of operation required is specified by pressing one of five further buttons; these buttons are marked $+$, $-$, $\times$, $\div$, and Z. The effect of pressing the Z button is to fill the accumulator with zeros. The other buttons cause the appropriate arithmetical operation to occur between the numbers in the register and the accumulator and the result is placed in the accumulator.

To illustrate the procedure, let us consider the steps in multiplying 57 by 39. We first put zero in the accumulator by pressing the Z button. The number 57 is set in the register. The $+$ button is pressed to cause the addition

$$57 + 0$$

and the answer, 57, appears in the accumulator. The number 39 is then set in the register and the $\times$ button is pressed to cause the desired multiplication, the result 2223 then appearing in the accumulator. The 57 is lost but 39 remains in the register.

Let us now make a list of the steps required for a more complicated calculation. The calculation is to multiply 17 by 18 and to multiply 19 by 20; add the answers together, and divide the result by 2. This list is as follows:

    (1) press Z
    (2) set 17 in the register
    (3) press $+$
    (4) set 18 in the register
    (5) press $\times$
    (6) copy result 306 from the accumulator on to paper
    (7) press Z
    (8) set 19 in the register
    (9) press $+$

(10) set 20 in the register
(11) press × (causing 380 to appear in the accumulator)
(12) set 306 (from paper) in the register
(13) press + (causing 686 to appear in the accumulator)
(14) set 2 in the register
(15) press ÷
(16) copy result 343 from the accumulator on to paper

The steps in this list are of three distinct types: (a) providing numerical information to the machine by setting numbers into the register, (b) indicating type of calculation by pressing +, −, ×, ÷, or Z button, and (c) removing numerical information from the machine by copying on to paper.

The calculation just considered could be performed much more readily if the machine had an extra register as in Fig. 1.2 and most present-day desk calculators have at least three registers, including the accumulator, with facilities for copying numbers from one register to another. This reduces the necessity to copy intermediate results on to paper.

We have so far considered only whole numbers in our calculations. Desk calculators can also handle decimals. This does not require any change in the internal mechanism but merely the fitting of pointers which can slide along the side of each register. In Fig. 1.2, we see the numbers 1·234 and 5·678 in the registers and the result of multiplying these together is seen in the accumulator, namely 7·006652. As far as the mechanism is concerned, the numbers are 1234 and 5678, the result of multiplication being 7006652. Incidentally, this multiplication shows why the accumulator is usually constructed with more available figures than the registers.

Fractions cannot be represented in the calculator but the equivalent decimal can be used, thus,

$$0 \cdot 5 \quad \text{represents } \tfrac{1}{2},$$
$$0 \cdot 25 \text{ represents } \tfrac{1}{4}.$$

In the case of

$$0 \cdot 333\ldots \text{ representing } \tfrac{1}{3},$$

it is necessary to limit the number of 3's according to the figures available in the register. For high accuracy,

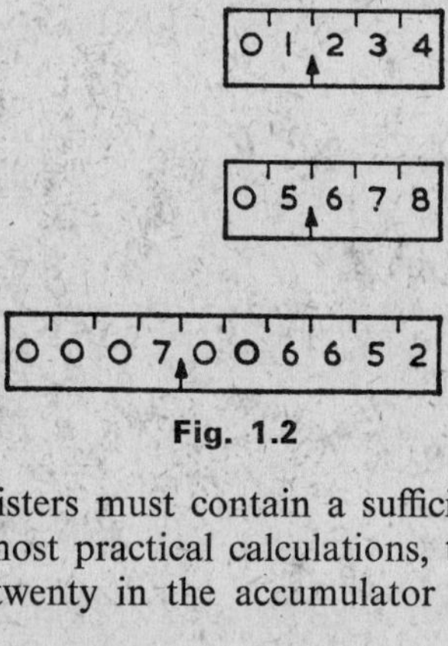

Fig. 1.2

therefore, registers must contain a sufficient number of figures. For most practical calculations, ten figures in a register and twenty in the accumulator are considered adequate.

Negative numbers are sometimes required in calculations. These arise in certain types of subtraction operation. Thus

$$5 - 3 = 2$$

but

$$3 - 5 = -2.$$

In using a desk calculator, negative numbers can usually be avoided by arranging the calculation appropriately. However, if this latter subtraction were attempted on our original calculator, the number

99999 99998

would appear in the accumulator. This is called the '9's complement' of 2. It is interesting to note that if we add 2 to it, we obtain

$$100000\ 00000.$$

Since the accumulator will only hold ten figures, the 1 is lost and we have zero, as we would expect since

$$-2 + 2 = 0.$$

In proceeding from the desk calculator to the electronic computer, the three types of step in a calculation must be mechanized. Steps of type (a) and (b) involve sending information to the computer and steps of type (c) involve receiving information from the computer. A computer must thus have a means of input and a means of output for information. In the earlier computers, two separate channels were used for type (a) and (b) information. This method would be very wasteful of time in an electronic computer since the time required to read the information would be large compared with the time of calculation. The difficulty is overcome by reading in all the type (a) and (b) information before the calculation is started, often using only one input channel. This, however, gives rise to the need for storage of information within the computer and this is provided by having many extra registers capable of holding either numbers or coded instructions which the computer can obey. Since 'register' is usually associated with numbers, the expression 'word of storage' is used in connection with computers. These registers are not visible on the exterior of the computer.

The desk calculator we first considered was imaginary and in a similar manner we shall now go on to study the operation of an imaginary electronic computer. But let us first pay a visit to an imaginary computer installation.

Electronic Computer

An electronic computer consists of a complex of electronic equipment which is usually housed in a pleasantly enamelled metal casing. There is at least one channel by which information can be given to the computer and at least one channel by which information can be received from the computer. The input channels are normally units for reading punched cards or punched paper tape. The output channels may be units for punching cards or paper tape or the computer may be attached to a printer which can print results directly on paper. We shall suppose that the computer has one input and one output using paper tape. There is usually a control desk with a limited number of buttons and switches and possibly a cathode ray tube display for showing the electrical states of circuits in the computer. The computer, when in proper working order, will be under the control of an operator who has the job of feeding work into it. This work will have been prepared by people called *programmers* working in offices away from the computer itself. For each item of work that the computer is required to do, a tape is prepared on which is a complete statement of the calculations required in a suitably coded form. This tape is sent by the programmer to a 'tape queue'. The computer operator takes the first tape from the queue and places the beginning of it in the tape reader. By pressing an appropriate 'start' button, the computer is put in a standard empty state and it then proceeds to read the tape. When the tape has been read, the computer gets on with the calculation and punches out results on the output tape punch. When it has finished the calculation and punched out all the results as indicated to the operator by a light, it waits for the operator to put in a new item of work. The operator does this after removing the length of tape which constitutes the output from the computer. This is sent back to the programmer together with the input tape. The programmer arranges for the output tape to be fed through a tape reader connected to a printer in order to obtain the results in the form of a printed sheet of paper.

This procedure may be disrupted by two possibilities. The first is that the computer may fail and no results are punched out. When this happens the maintenance engineer takes over and endeavours to rectify the fault. The second possibility is that the input tape may be erroneous so that no results, or else erroneous results, are obtained from the computer. This usually happens when input tapes are first prepared and it is important for the programmer to test his tape by using it for some simple but typical calculations, which can be checked by a desk calculating machine.

Mode of Operation of an Electronic Computer

It is not necessary for the programmer or user to understand the electronic circuits which make up the working parts of a computer. However, a brief outline of the general working is necessary and this will now be given.

Fig. 1.3 shows our computer in diagrammatic form, as the user sees it. In this figure we see a number of rectangles which represent the storage system of the computer. When the computer reads the input tape, the information is taken in and is held in the storage system, which may be of a magnetic or electrical nature. This information is used by the computer in performing the calculations. The elements of storage, represented by rectangles in Fig. 1.3, will be referred to as *words*. An important element of storage, standing by itself, is the accumulator, which is used in performing arithmetic operations as in a desk calculator. The remaining storage is divided into a special store and a main store, and together these have 1000 words which are numbered in sequence as shown. Actual computers have considerably more words of storage.

The information that can be stored in the computer is of two distinct types. One type is numerical information

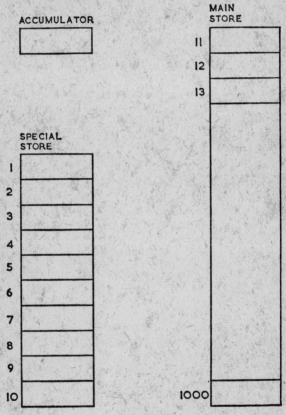

Fig. 1.3

in the form of numbers. We shall suppose that all numbers can be expressed with up to ten figures, with the decimal point occurring at either end or anywhere in between. If the decimal point is at the right hand end, the number will be a whole number or *integer*. Numbers may be positive or negative. The other type of information is used to tell the computer what arithmetical operations it must perform on the numbers. This information consists of a series of discrete *orders* which the computer can understand. We shall be describing these orders in more detail below but at present we note that one order is stored in a word of the store.

The words of the main store can be used to hold either numbers or orders. This is also true of the accumulator. The words of the special store can be used to hold numbers only and these numbers must be integers either positive or negative.

Computer Orders

An order consists of two parts called the *function* and the *address*. The function will be denoted by a capital letter and the address is a number. Sometimes the address part of the order is irrelevant. This is so in the case of the first function we shall describe.

An order with function Z, when obeyed by the computer, causes the accumulator to contain the number zero. Any number previously held in the accumulator disappears.

An order with function A causes a number to be added to the number in the accumulator and the result is held in the accumulator. The number previously in the accumulator disappears. The particular number added is taken from one of the words of the store. This word is the one whose sequence number is the same as the address of the A order. For example, if word 273 contains the number

5·327, then the order

$$A \ 273$$

causes 5·327 to be added into the accumulator. When this operation is performed the 5·327 also stays in word 273 which thus remains unaltered. In general let us denote the address of an order by n and let us denote the contents of word n by $C(n)$. Let us denote the accumulator by a and its contents by $C(a)$. Then we can say that the order

$$A \ n$$

causes $C(a) + C(n)$ to be placed in a, all other words of the store remaining unchanged.

The subtraction order

$$S \ n$$

causes $C(a) - C(n)$ to be placed in a, all other words of the store remaining unchanged.

The multiplication order

$$M \ n$$

causes $C(a) \times C(n)$ to be placed in a, all other words of the store remaining unchanged.

The division order

$$D \ n$$

causes $C(a) \div C(n)$ to be placed in a, all other words of the store remaining unchanged.

We now have orders to do all the basic arithmetic operations. Another order is required to remove the result from the accumulator to a word in the store. This is the remove order

$$R \ n$$

which causes $C(a)$ to be placed in word n, the accumulator and all other words of the store remaining unchanged. The original contents of word n disappear.

There is one other function that we shall describe at this stage. This is E, which indicates that the calculation is complete. It causes the computer to stop and a light shines on the control desk to inform the operator. As in the case of Z, the address of an E order is irrelevant. There are five other functions that we shall consider a little later. We shall turn our attention now to writing down lists of orders to cause the computer to carry out some simple arithmetic.

Simple Arithmetical Procedures

A list of orders to cause the computer to perform a calculation is called a *program*. This list must be stored in the computer so that the orders occupy consecutive words of the main store. For definiteness we shall regard the list as occupying words 11, 12, 13 and so on.

Let us consider this sequence of orders:

$$11:Z \qquad ,$$
$$12:A \qquad 1,$$
$$13:A \qquad 2,$$
$$14:R \qquad 3,$$
$$15:E \qquad ,$$

Here, the number on the left indicates the number of the word in which the order is stored. The spacing of the numbers and letters is for neatness of appearance and has no significance as far as the computer is concerned. The comma after every order has a significance but we shall not concern ourselves with it at present. The effect of the list of orders can be understood by considering the state of the storage after each order has been obeyed. The first order causes zero to be placed in the accumulator. The second order adds in the number in word 1 so that we then have $C(1)$ in the accumulator. The third order adds in the number in word 2, giving $C(1) + C(2)$ in the accumulator. The fourth order removes this sum to be stored in word 3. Finally an E order indicates the end of the calculation.

We shall next consider the orders corresponding to the steps given earlier for the desk calculation. We shall suppose that to start, the numbers are stored as follows:

17 in word 1,
18 in word 2,
19 in word 3,
20 in word 4,
2 in word 5.

A suitable sequence of orders would then be:

11:Z   ,
12:A   1,
13:M   2,
14:R   6,
15:Z   ,
16:A   3,
17:M   4,
18:A   6,
19:D   5,
20:R   7,
21:E   ,

The effect of this sequence is to calculate 17×18 and put the result in word 6. Word 6 is here used as a temporary location for part of the computation and corresponds to the paper used with the desk calculator. Words so used are referred to as *working space*. The multiplication 19×20 is performed by the order in word 17. After the addition of the previous result from word 6, the division in word 19 produces the result 343 which is then removed to word 7.

As a further example, let us consider the conversion of Centigrade temperatures to Fahrenheit. To do this we multiply by $\frac{9}{5}$ and add 32. For example 15°C is 59°F. Let us suppose that originally $\frac{9}{5}$ (i.e., 1·8) is stored in word 101 and number 32 is stored in word 102. The Centigrade temperature to be converted we shall suppose to be in word 103. The list of orders is:

$$
\begin{array}{lll}
11{:}Z & & ,\\
12{:}A & 101, \\
13{:}M & 103, \\
14{:}A & 102, \\
15{:}R & 104, \\
16{:}E & & ,
\end{array}
$$

and the resulting Fahrenheit temperature appears in word 104.

Finally, we shall consider the evaluation of a simple algebraic formula, but this example can be omitted by readers not familiar with algebra. Let us evaluate the expression

$$z = \frac{x(x + y)}{x - (y/x)}$$

where x stands for the number in word 200, y stands for the number in word 201, and the result z is required to be placed in word 202. A suitable sequence of orders would be:

$$
\begin{array}{lll}
11{:}Z & & ,\\
12{:}A & 201, \\
13{:}D & 200, \\
14{:}R & 203, \\
15{:}Z & & ,\\
16{:}A & 200, \\
17{:}S & 203, \\
18{:}R & 203, \\
19{:}Z & & ,\\
20{:}A & 200, \\
21{:}A & 201, \\
22{:}M & 200,
\end{array}
$$

$$23:D \quad 203,$$
$$24:R \quad 202,$$
$$25:E \qquad ,$$

The effect of this sequence is as follows. After clearing the accumulator, y/x is calculated and is placed in word 203 by the order in word 14. The next step is to calculate $x - y/x$, which is placed in word 203 by the order in word 18. x and y are added together by the orders in words 20 and 21. The next order puts

$$x(x + y)$$

in the accumulator and the next forms the required expression for z.

Input and Output Arrangements

In our last example, we assumed that the values x and y were already present in words 200 and 201. These values would in fact be taken in off the input tape. The input and output of numbers are effected by two orders which are as follows.

The input order

$$I \; n$$

causes one number to be read from the tape in the tape reader and it is placed in word n. The original contents of word n disappear.

The output order

$$O \; n$$

causes the number in word n to be punched on the output tape. The contents of word n remain unaltered.

The input of the orders to the computer is done automatically and so no particular arrangement need be made for this by the programmer.

We can now look more closely at the tape which the programmer must provide. Fig. 1.4 shows a typical piece of tape. Standard teleprinter tape is 0·7 inch wide and this is used in many computers. There is a line of small circular holes in the tape which is used to move the tape through the tape reader by means of a sprocket wheel. Apart from this there is room for five holes across the tape and these holes may or may not be punched out. This gives 32 possibilities for the combination of holes in a row. When only the sprocket hole is punched, we regard the tape as blank and blank tape is ignored by the computer. A manual tape punch has 32 keys and by depressing the appropriate key, any desired combination of

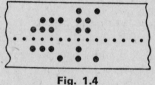

Fig. 1.4

holes can be punched on a tape. A manual tape punch for use with our computer would have the keys marked with the integers 0 to 9, the capital letters representing the functions and also the following six marks

$$: , ( ) . /$$

The input tape would start with blank tape, then would follow the program composed of the orders to the computer. These would be followed by any numbers required for the calculation and finally there would be an ending of blank tape. The numbers required for the calculation are collectively referred to as the *data*. The tape is marked to show which end is the beginning and is usually kept rolled up. The following is a complete tape for the first programming example given above.

$$11{:}I \qquad 1,$$
$$12{:}I \qquad 2,$$

```
13:Z      ,
14:A      1,
15:A      2,
16:R      3,
17:O      3,
18:E      /
        2·53,
        7·18,
```

We shall consider what happens when this tape is put in the tape reader and the start button is pressed. The tape is read in and the orders are deposited in the words indicated by the numbers on the left. The comma indicates to the computer where one order ends and the next begins. After the last order we see the sign /. This tells the computer that all the program has been read in and at this point the tape stops. The computer then starts to obey orders starting at a definite word in the store. We shall suppose from now on that this word is word 11, so all programs must have their first order in this position. When the computer obeys the order in word 11, it takes in a number from the tape. Since the tape stopped after the / mark, the number read in is the next group of characters on the tape, i.e., 2·53. The comma indicates the end of the number. This value 2·53 is placed in word 1. The order in word 12 causes the 7·18 to be taken in and stored in word 2. The calculation then proceeds as before and finally the order in word 17 causes the result to be punched on the output tape.

Conditional and Unconditional Jumps

In the examples we have considered so far, the computer starts obeying a list of orders and proceeds directly through the list arriving at the E order at the bottom. In more complicated programs it is often necessary to cause the computer to stop obeying the orders in sequence and obey next the order in a different part of the store. This can be effected by an unconditional jump order

$$J\ n$$

which causes the order in word n to be obeyed next followed by the orders in words $n + 1$, $n + 2$ and so on.

There are two conditional jump orders which depend on the number in the accumulator. The order

$$K\ n$$

causes a jump, like J, if the number in the accumulator is positive or zero. But if the number in the accumulator is negative, there is no jump and the orders continue to be obeyed in sequence.

The order

$$L\ n$$

causes a jump, like J, if the number in the accumulator is zero. But if this number is not zero, there is no jump and the orders continue to be obeyed in sequence.

The conditional jump orders enable the computer to take elementary decisions. They can be used to build up programs for far more complicated decision taking.

We have now described all the functions in our imaginary computer. Using these few functions, programs for the most complicated mathematical calculations can be constructed. There is one more feature of our computer that we must introduce. It is useful, as we shall see later, for the computer to be able to modify an order before it is obeyed. This can be done if the order is followed by a number in brackets, for example,

$$M\ n\ (m)$$

where m stands for an integer from 1 to 10 inclusive. The effect of this is that before the order is obeyed, the address becomes

$$n + C(m).$$

That is, the number in word m is added to n to form the new address. This addition takes place in a separate part of the computer and the contents of the word containing the order remain unchanged as M n (m).

Magnetic Tape and Discs

In our account of computer programming we have referred to the computer store which holds the program and numbers used in performing calculations. The numbers and letters involved are stored as coded electrical or magnetic signals. Since letters can be stored, it follows that complete words and sentences can also be read into the computer and stored by using a modified input order. Such information can also be output from the computer. This facility is essential in business applications where lists of materials or names and addresses may be stored in the computer for subsequent output. Such lists can be sorted into alphabetical order by an appropriate computer program.

The computer store, as we have considered it so far, is fixed within the computer and is of limited capacity. In many business applications it is necessary to store vast amounts of information for computer use and for this purpose, some auxiliary form of storage is needed. The earliest type of auxiliary storage was *magnetic tape*. A tape store is similar in appearance to a tape recorder. A high quality of tape is required and about eight tracks of information can be placed on a half-inch wide tape; one of the tracks usually being a marker track to indicate the position of the tape. Tape units are available which can move the tape in one direction only, while others are capable of moving the tape backwards and forwards to search for a particular position. Such searching is, needless to say, extremely slow. Information can be 'written' on to the tape by the computer. The tape can then be removed and kept for later use when the information can be 'read' back from the tape into the computer store.

The last few years have seen a rapid development of *magnetic discs* as a means of large capacity storage. The latest systems resemble gramophones in many respects. The discs have a recording surface, in the same way as a gramophone record and a twelve-inch diameter disc will store about half a million characters (i.e., letters or figures). The recording surface is enclosed in plastic. The discs are removable and are mounted on a turntable but the speed of rotation is 1200 revolutions per minute. The tracks on the recording surface are concentric circles and a particular track is selected by a single, movable reading head. It will be apparent that a particular position on a disc can be found far more quickly than in the case of magnetic tape. As yet, however, disc stores are elaborate and expensive items.

The computer store will be referred to as the *high-speed store* to distinguish it from the slower forms of auxiliary storage.

Computers Large and Small

Computers vary considerably in size and store capacity as well as in speed of operation, depending upon the application. Before long, computers will be available which will fit into a coat pocket. At the present time, the smallest computer for business use will stand on a table and is the size of a typewriter. Its cost is £1680, the cheapest computer on the market. For a somewhat higher cost, a variety of computers are available, the size of desks, for performing many routine clerical operations. At the other end of the scale, large computers costing half a million pounds or more, are being installed by many companies to deal with all aspects of the business. A computer of this type requires a large room which must be kept clean and is air-conditioned. The computer is seen not as a single entity but as a set of 'units' standing separately in the room and apparently in isolation from each other. The units are in fact joined together by under-floor wiring. The computer consists of a *central processing unit* where the arithmetical calculations are performed and where the high-speed store of the computer is situated. The other units are collectively referred to as *peripheral equipment* and may include magnetic tape or disc stores, tape or card readers for input, tape or card punches for output, and also a high-speed printer to give readable output on paper. Other units can be attached for particular applications. There will also be a desk from which the overall operation of the computer is controlled. The control desk and input and output equipment need not be located with the rest of the computer; indeed, it is becoming possible to have two or more control positions connected by cables to the one computer and the computer's time is shared between the requirements of the various control positions. Such *multi-access* arrangements are becoming important in business applications.

Jobs on Computers

The operation of a large computer requires staff of several types.

Computer operators are required to control the operation of the computer. In addition to minding the control desk, the computer must be kept supplied with input information in the form of punched cards or tape. The computer output, in the form of punched cards or tape or printed paper, must also be removed and dispatched. It may be necessary to remove and replace magnetic tapes or discs. If the high speed, at which a computer is capable of working, is to be effectively utilized, a very efficient clerical system must be maintained for receiving work, processing and dispatching it. One of the reasons for multi-access development was to avoid congestion in the flow of work through a single control position.

Operators are also required for the card and tape punches which are used to produce the punched cards or paper tape by which all information must be put into the computer. While equipment has been developed so that computers can read printed documents, it is still not possible for a computer to read handwriting. Hence the need to convert such writing into punched cards or tape. The punches are fitted with keyboards, like a typewriter, and the resulting cards or tape can be fed into a printer to obtain a readable version of the information for comparison with the original.

The *maintenance engineer* is needed to repair faults which may occur in the computer. In order to get the most out of a computer it must be in operation twenty-four hours per day, but of this a limited period is set aside for routine maintenance procedures. The possibility of computer breakdown must be borne in mind in all computer applications. The advent of transistor electronics has, however, greatly reduced the likelihood of such failures.

The *data processing manager* supervises the computer staff and ensures the smooth working of the whole system.

This is the complete team, in cases where only routine and well-proven uses of the computer are involved. In such cases, the programs used by the computer will be stored on cards or paper tape for input to the computer when required. Alternatively, programs may be kept in magnetic storage.

Few computer installations for business applications have reached this final state of perfection, mainly because schemes for computer use are constantly being improved upon. In these circumstances, the staff will also include systems analysts and programmers.

The *systems analyst* is responsible for devising schemes to implement the desires of the management regarding projected uses of the computer. He must be able to talk to the management, explaining the limitations of the computer in language which is intelligible to them. Once the main outlines of a new scheme are settled, he must then prepare a detailed statement of exactly what the computer is to do. The usual form of this statement is the *flow chart*, in which each statement detail is equivalent to a few computer orders. The implementation of a new computer scheme inevitably involves changes to the existing staff organization of the company and it is the duty of the systems analyst to propose the necessary changes in staff and procedures. This in turn may require training schemes to prepare the staff for their new duties.

The *programmer* has the job of transcribing the flow chart, provided by the systems analyst, into a computer program. The programmer works in an office away from the computer and when he wishes to run his program on the computer, he sends it to the operating staff with appropriate instructions. It will usually require several trial runs before all mistakes have been removed from the program. When the program has been thoroughly tested, the new computer scheme can be implemented. In writing his program, the programmer can use the basic code of the computer, as was explained earlier in this chapter. It is more likely however that he will use a special *programming language*. A number of such languages exist, the aim of which is to make programs simpler to write. The computer can then be made to translate the program, so written, into its own basic code. The programmer must be painstaking and meticulous, no matter what language he uses.

At the present time, schemes for computer use are far from perfect and many schemes which are satisfactory are in the process of improvement. This has given rise to a demand for systems analysts and programmers which greatly exceeds the supply and this situation is expected to continue into the seventies.

In addition to the jobs described above, which exist at all computer installations, specialist staff are employed by computer manufacturing firms on research into new computer techniques, on the design of new computers and on the manufacture, assembly, sale and installation of current models.

Data Transmission Facilities

In the computer centre outlined above, the work arrives at the centre and is dispatched from it in the form of printed or written documents or as punched cards or paper tape. Such items can be conveniently sent through the post to distant users but the delay in posting to and from the centre may materially reduce the value of the results in some applications. Where data processing is needed urgently, it may be useful to connect the distant station by cable to the computer centre. This can be done most conveniently by means of telegraph and telephone lines.

During the last few years, the demand for facilities which will enable digital data for computers to be transmitted over telephone and telegraph lines has greatly increased. The GPO has kept in close touch with this development and regards facilities for data transmission as of such importance to the nation's commercial, business and industrial undertakings as to merit their

establishment as a separate group of communications
services known as *Datel Services.* Datel Services are a combination of a particular type of line and, where necessary,
a *modem* (short for modulator–demodulator) unit to provide a customer with a data transmission facility in a
stated speed range. Speeds are measured in 'bits per
second'. A 'bit' is a hole in a card or paper tape and five
such bits are needed for a character (i.e., a letter or figure).
Thus Datel 100 Service can transmit 100 bits per second
which is 20 characters per second.

Datel 100 Service is provided by telegraph lines which,
it will be remembered, are used normally for the transmission of telegrams. No modem is required. Transmission can be effected through the Telex System, which is
a switched public teleprinter system, or alternatively
through a private telegraph line connecting two stations.
The normal method of communication is by means of
teleprinters but data transmission from and to five-hole
paper tape can be effected. Normal speed is 50 bits per
second, with 100 bits per second by special arrangement.

Datel 200, 300 and 600 Services are provided by telephone lines, an appropriate modem being used for the
speed which the customer requires. The modem is located
in the customer's premises and is connected to the telephone line and to the customer's *terminal equipment*
which may consist of a card or tape reader or punch and
error detecting devices. By setting up a normal telephone
call and, when contact has been established, switching
over to the modem and terminal equipment, data can be
transmitted to any similarly equipped telephone. Transmission in both directions can take place simultaneously
if required. There are no extra charges for data transmission calls; customers pay only the normal telephone call
charges and, of course, full use can be made of cheap
rates and contract calls. Private telephone lines can be

provided offering the same facilities. To meet the needs of customers with a network of data transmission lines, the GPO, as part of the Datel Service, can supply special switching and line concentration arrangements for data terminals at a computer centre.

Datel 2000 Service is provided over private telephone lines at an extra charge. At the time of writing, suitable modems are under development but are not yet available from the Post Office.

It will be seen, then, that the problem of transmitting data for computers over long distances is well in hand and the 600 service is already available for connections to the U.S.A. and Europe. This facility has an obvious use in connecting the divisions of an international business organization and in enabling up to the minute information to be available at the headquarters. The same applies to chain stores and bank branches.

We have already seen how the multi-access facility on a computer enables distant users to have access to it. A logical extension to this idea is the possibility of connecting two computers together by Datel Service for the purpose of passing information from the store of one computer to that of the other. Finally, the possibility exists of having a 'grid' of computers interconnected by transmission lines. A user could then be channelled to a free computer to obtain immediate service. The 'grid' concept, while attractive, will require further research and is unlikely to materialize in the next few years.

Business Applications

We have so far considered a computer as if it were the property of a company and operated entirely under the company's control. In many cases this is so but it is not the only way in which computers can aid the business world. An alternative is the *computer bureau* which is a special company which owns or hires a computer but specializes entirely in doing work for other companies. Such bureaux serve a useful purpose as many firms are too small to justify a computer and its specialized staff. They can, nonetheless, have the advantage of the latest computer methods through the staff of the bureau. Larger firms also make use of bureaux prior to installing their own computer or for the purpose of trying out new schemes during phases of expansion.

In the following chapters we shall examine those areas of business where computers appear to have established themselves as aids to efficiency. As the whole subject is in a rapid state of expansion, it is clearly impossible to assess at this stage the place which computers will eventually occupy and to what extent they will alter the nature and conduct of the business world. Some applications of computers may seem extremely simple, in principle at least, and it may appear to the reader that a computer is not actually necessary in some cases. The point to be borne in mind, however, is that once the cost of a computer has been justified by a number of worthwhile applications, the company can then use it on a variety of other tasks which may not of themselves justify the services of a computer.

2 Payroll

In spite of the progress of automation, there is still no organization, public or private, which can operate entirely without human labour. It follows then, that in every organization the need arises to calculate and pay out wages. These tasks are collectively referred to as *payroll*.

The payment of wages for human labour is a feature of economic systems of every political flavour from capitalist to communist. Exceptions do occur in the case of some village communities based on primitive agriculture. In the Fiji Islands, for example, the villages continue to thrive without the use of money and in spite of the proximity of modern towns. But with a few limited exceptions of this type, it may be said that payroll calculations are a necessary part of human activity throughout the world. The application of computers to these calculations is thus a clear benefit in that it lifts the drudgery of the work from the minds of men. In view of the almost universal occurrence of payroll in human activities, it follows that this is likely to become the most widespread application of computers in the business world. It is fitting then that we should start our study of computers in business with this application.

In Britain, the first computer to be applied to business calculations was used for payroll and, at present, payroll is the most widespread computer application. In the

U.S.A., on the other hand, payroll has so far lagged behind some other applications.

Nature of the Calculation

While the payment of wages for labour would seem a simple enough concept, a number of factors conspire to complicate the issue. In the first place, rates of pay are not uniform. Indeed, with the diversification of trades in a modern industrial society, a great variety of types of work have developed, each with its own rate of pay; an individual worker may receive several different rates during one week of work. Overtime working adds to the variety of pay rates. A second complicating factor is the increasing tendency throughout the world for governments to extract taxes from the worker's pay packet before he receives it. The work involved in this extraction is made the responsibility of the employer. With the passage of time, a particular tax tends to become more complicated owing to modifications and exceptions introduced by the Government in the light of changing national circumstances. Finally, the payroll calculation involves the deduction of amounts from the pay packet in accordance with the wishes of the worker. These deductions may be for such things as savings schemes, holiday pay or sports club.

The net effect of these complicating factors is that the clerical work involved in the preparation of the payroll becomes exaggerated out of all proportion to the number of employees. Employers complain, perhaps with some justification, that they subsidize the Inland Revenue and act as unpaid unofficial tax collectors although this earns them no thanks from the income tax authorities, or their own employees. The fact remains, however, that paying its employees accurately and on time is an obligation of any business. Reliability is a basic essential. On the other hand, the time, effort and expense of the operation contributes nothing to the productivity or service of the business.

Having outlined the problem in general terms, we shall now proceed to look a little more closely at the payroll calculation as we have it in Britain today. Traditionally, wages and salaries are paid either weekly or monthly. To avoid confusion we shall restrict our attention to monthly pay. Although weekly payments do not materially alter the payroll calculation, the increased frequency of payment clearly adds to the work of the pay office. The basis of payment to the employee may be a basic monthly wage together with overtime and possibly other allowances. Alternatively, the entire pay may be calculated by hourly rates from a time sheet which has been filled in by the employee, stating the number of hours he has worked on specific tasks. By either method, the total amount due to the employee for the month is calculated and is referred to as his *gross pay*. As an example, Sam Jones, a sheet metal worker, submits a time sheet for January stating that during the month he has worked 140 hours at the standard rate and 20 hours overtime. The standard rate is £0·50 per hour and the overtime rate is £0·75 per hour. In addition, Sam receives a lodging allowance of £15 for the month. His gross pay is thus

$$(140 \times 0·50) + (20 \times 0·75) + 15$$

which is £100.

Having arrived at the gross pay for an employee, it is then necessary to subtract his deductions. These divide into voluntary and compulsory categories. The voluntary deductions, approved by the employee for his own convenience, usually consist of fixed amounts each month. Each month, Sam Jones pays £5 to the works saving scheme, £5 for holiday saving and £0·40 to the sports club. His total voluntary deductions are thus £10·40. The compulsory deductions consist of three types of tax, namely, *income tax*, *national insurance* and *graduated pensions scheme*. The reason for the three types is that the latter two are intended to contribute specifically to the future welfare of the employee, whereas income tax is intended as a payment towards the expenses of the state. The national insurance contribution is a fixed monthly payment of which a proportion is paid by the employee and the rest by the employer. The money collected in this way goes to provide payments to unemployed and sick workers. The graduated pension scheme contribution also is paid partly by the employee and partly by the employer. The amount is a percentage of the gross pay and the money collected goes to provide a pension for the employee. The graduated pension scheme is optional, in that the employee may be allowed instead to participate in some private form of pension scheme. The calculation of income tax will be mentioned in a later section of this chapter. In the case of Sam Jones, his national insurance contraction is £3 per month and the employer pays £10. He pays 5 per cent of his gross pay to the graduated pension scheme and the employer puts the same amount (i.e., £5 each). His income tax in January is £12. His total compulsory deductions are thus

$$3 + 5 + 12$$

or £20.

The subtraction of the voluntary and compulsory deductions from the gross pay gives the amount of money actually received by the employee for the month. It is referred to as his *net pay*. For Sam Jones it is

$$100 - 10·40 - 20$$

or £69·60. The employer must pay Sam this amount.
Also the employer must send £12 to the income tax
authorities, £13 to the national insurance fund and £10
to the graduated pension fund.

When the payroll calculation has been performed,
either manually or by computer, the necessary cash must
be obtained from the bank and the pay packets made up
in time to be collected on pay day. The tax payments are
usually made by cheque. Many workers also choose to
be paid by cheque but in the following description we
shall only consider the procedure when the payment is
by cash.

The use of a computer for payroll is most effective
where there are large numbers of employees who draw
fairly standard wages. The computer has been found less
satisfactory for small numbers of employees or in cases
where the wages vary violently and erratically from
month to month. This is an instance of the general rule
that a computer can most readily handle large numbers
of routine procedures but is inefficient if the number of
exceptional procedures becomes appreciable.

Westminster Bank Payroll Service

A firm which does not possess its own computer can
have its payroll calculations performed by a computer
bureau. Such a payroll service is offered by Westminster
Bank. There are innumerable variations of payroll procedures and before designing this service, the methods
used by representative industrial and commercial organizations were studied. The system which emerged as a
result has a high degree of flexibility and should readily
accommodate the requirements of most firms.

Once a firm has agreed to use the payroll service, a
carrying case is provided and this is used for the transfer of written and printed information between the firm

and the bank's payroll office in London. Once each
month the case goes from the firm to the payroll office.
The information in it is used in the calculation of the
month's payroll and the printed computer output is
returned to the firm in time for pay day. In the event of
a computer breakdown, the bank has similar computers
elsewhere which can be used.

Let us now look more closely at the information which
is transmitted. Before starting to use the service, a firm
fills in a basic record card for each employee. These cards
are provided by the bank and there are spaces on them
for a variety of information about the employee, e.g.,
name, rates of pay, tax code and entitled allowances.
This information about the employee is of the type
which will not normally change from one month to the
next. The firm must also allocate to each employee a
payroll number from a sequence of numbers specified by
the bank. The set of basic record cards are sent to the
payroll service. Here the information is punched into
cards for input to the computer. An appropriate program is used in the computer to transfer the information on the cards to a magnetic tape. This magnetic tape
forms the basis of all future calculations. The allocation
of a payroll number to each employee enables his information to be readily located on the magnetic record, in
the subsequent computer calculations. A further computer program is used to print out all this basic information from the magnetic tape to ensure that the magnetic record is correct in every detail.

The information sent by the firm each month consists
of two parts. First there is information relating to changes
in the basic records. Such changes include employees
leaving, new employees starting and alterations to rates of
pay for existing employees. Secondly there is the information relating to the particular month. This includes the

number of hours worked by each employee, details of overtime and any unusual payments such as productivity bonuses. The bank provides the stationery upon which all this information must be presented in a specified manner. This facilitates the immediate punching of the information into cards as soon as it arrives at the payroll office.

In performing the payroll calculation each month, the computer makes use of the basic record on magnetic tape and the cards into which the current month information has been punched. The end product of the calculation is a new basic record tape, which includes all up-to-date modifications, and the computer printout which is returned to the firm. The necessary stationery for the next month's information is dispatched at the same time.

The printout consists of a list of the employees with details of the pay calculation for each, together with a mention of any amendments to the basic record. Also printed is a pay slip or pay envelope for each employee. A *cash analysis* states the total number of bank notes and coins of each denomination which are needed to make up the payments. In addition, printed tables can be provided giving, for example, total hours worked at the various rates of pay, or total deductions to taxes and other funds. At quarterly or annual intervals, statements are printed of taxes paid by each employee. Such statements must be sent to the tax authorities and to each employee. If the firm chooses to divide its employees into departments, the printed output from the computer can be similarly divided with appropriate departmental headings.

Any changes in rates of tax, as introduced by the Government from time to time, are dealt with by a modification to the computer programs. Being a bank, Westminster's payroll service can offer certain other

facilities, particularly where employees choose to be paid
by cheque. We shall leave discussion of this matter until
we consider banking in Chapter 5.

Operation of the Computer

As we have seen, the basic records for the payroll calculation are stored in magnetic form on tape. This tape is
kept on a reel which is stored in a plastic container to
exclude dust. When the information is required by the
computer, the reel must be fitted on to a magnetic tape
unit associated with the computer. The tape is threaded
through the reading head of the unit and is wound on to
a further reel just as in the case of a tape recorder. When
the unit is set working, under the control of the computer, the tape winds from one reel to the other and as it
passes the reading head, the stored information is transferred into the high-speed store of the computer. The
information in the high-speed store is always available
for use by the computer but the information stored on
tape is only available after the tape has been moved so
that the required portion is in the reading head. This is
a time-consuming operation, by computer speeds, so it is
usual for computer programs to be arranged so that
the information on a magnetic tape is called for in the
sequence in which it is stored. This gives rise to the idea
of a *computer run*. A computer run consists of setting
one or more reels of magnetic tape on the computer's
tape units, after which the computer uses the information
on the tapes and may at the same time transfer information on to one or more new tapes. To an observer, the
reels of tape appear to rotate more or less together until
all the tape has been consumed. The reels are then
re-wound and their removal from the computer's tape
units completes the run. During the course of the run,
the reels may start and stop as information is required

by the computer, depending on the progress of the calculation.

When information on a tape is merely read by the computer, this information remains unchanged after the run and so the reel can be removed for later use. On the other hand, when the purpose of the program is to alter the information of a tape, the usual procedure is to transfer the altered information to a new tape. This means that for any particular tape involved in the run, information is transferred in one direction only, either from tape to computer or vice versa. The result is that the 'old' tape is unchanged at the end of the run and can be retained, if desired, for record purposes. The 'new' tape is available for further use. It is usual to retain three or more generations of old tapes as a precaution against computer errors. Old tapes can then be re-used, the computer merely overwriting the old information with new.

Where the amount of information to be stored on a tape is too large for one reel, it is possible to continue on further reels. For this reason, a *magnetic file* is often referred to. A magnetic file consists of one or more reels of tape depending on the amount of information to be stored.

Computer programs are frequently stored on magnetic tape.

For business purposes, the usual type of computer output is the high-speed page printer. This prints on paper provided as a continuous sheet. A typical width of the sheet is fourteen inches. The sheet is divided into 'pages' by perforations, say nine inches apart. Along the edges of the sheet are sprocket holes to ensure correct movement of the paper by the printer. The printer prints lines of characters which are perpendicular to the length of the sheet, so that the pages have perforations at the top and bottom and sprocket holes down the sides. The characters are usually numbers or letters of the alphabet. In addition to the line by line printing, the computer can also direct the printer to start a new page. This enables the output information to be conveniently divided by tearing the perforations.

Pages of the size mentioned above are suitable when the output is in the form of a printed table but for many applications such pages would be wasteful. Pay slips, for example, could be printed on sheets, one quarter the size. The difficulty is overcome by having special paper for pay slips which in addition to the page perforations also has extra perforations dividing the page into four. This special paper can be preprinted with remarks such as 'gross pay' and 'net pay' with printed rectangles into which the computer can print the amounts. Where a large volume of output is to be dealt with, it is usually guillotined by a machine to produce the individual pay slips and in this case the sprocket holes are cut away. A further elaboration is to build envelopes on to the back of the paper so that the pay slip also becomes the pay envelope. This option is available at Westminster.

Income Tax

In this section we shall consider what is involved in the calculation of income tax by computer, but this may conveniently be omitted by readers not requiring an exercise in algebra.

The calculation is, of course, essentially the same whether by computer or not but for calculation by human beings a set of tables is provided by the tax office to simplify the arithmetic. The calculation is designed to smooth the payment of tax by the employee, over the course of the year, even though his pay may fluctuate from month to month. If the fluctuations became too violent they may result in a negative tax payment in a particular month, which is in fact a refund. However the total amount of tax paid during the year is related to the total annual income of the employee. Thus before proceeding to consider monthly tax payments we shall look at the total annual payment.

The financial year begins on 1st April and the income tax year begins on 6th April. The income tax year is essentially the same as the financial year but it allows a few days so that end of year payments may be settled before the tax for the year is calculated. (This is more applicable to taxes on companies than to income tax.)

Of the employee's total annual income, a certain amount of tax-free pay is allowed depending on his personal circumstances, but the calculation of this amount is not part of the payroll calculation. It is undertaken by the tax office and is conveyed from there to the employer. Of the remaining pay, a certain fraction of it is tax-free and is called 'earned income relief'. It is based on the notion that income which has been earned is more worthy than income which is unearned, such as interest on investments. At the time of writing, the fraction is $\frac{2}{9}$. The remaining pay is liable for tax.

Let I be the employee's total annual income and let F be the tax-free pay depending on personal circumstances. Let e be the fraction of earned income relief. Then the pay T liable for tax is given by

$$T = (I - F)(1 - e).$$

Let us suppose that the rate of tax is a fraction r. Thus if $r = 0.25$, this means that £0·25 of every pound is paid in tax. Thus the tax t on the amount T is given by

$$t = rT.$$

This is the total tax paid by the employee for the year.

We can now proceed to the monthly tax payments. Smoothing of the employee's income is effected by considering the total amount he has earned since the begin-

ning of the financial year. Let us consider the situation for
month m of the financial year. Thus if $m = 3$ we are considering the month of June. Let g_m be the employee's
gross pay for month m and let I_m be his total income from
the beginning of the financial year up to and including
month m. Then it follows from these definitions that

$$I_m = I_{m-1} + g_m.$$

We divide the tax-free pay F into twelve equal parts and
allocate a part to each month. Denoting such a part by
f, we have

$$F = 12f.$$

The tax-free pay F_m allocated to the first m months is thus
given by

$$F_m = mf.$$

Then the pay T_m liable for tax during the first m months is

$$T_m = (I_m - F_m)(1 - e)$$

and the tax on this pay is t_m given by

$$t_m = rT_m.$$

This is the total tax for the first m months. The amount of
tax to be paid in month m is thus given by

$$t_m - t_{m-1}.$$

The performance of this calculation for month m
requires the quantities $e, r, f, I_{m-1}, t_{m-1}, g_m$ to be known.
Of these, e and r are fixed from time to time by the Government and are the same for all employees. The quantity
f is particular to the individual employee. It is provided
by the tax office and usually it remains unchanged
throughout the financial year. The quantities I_{m-1}, t_{m-1}
must be carried forward from month to month for each
employee. The gross pay for the month, g_m, is derived
in the payroll calculation.

The above account of income tax is a simplification of

the current British system in that the rate of tax r has been assumed to be a constant. In fact, there are three rates of tax which are arranged so that the value of r in fact increases with the amount of taxable income. This precludes the possibility of using the above simple formula for t_m.

Payroll Programming

The payroll calculation offers us an opportunity to consider further the construction of computer programs. For this purpose we must extend our set of computer orders to deal with punched card input, page printer output and magnetic tape.

The cards used with computers are like postcards but normally have one of the corners clipped off. In a large stack of cards, this enables one to see at a glance that all of the cards are the right way up and the right way round. A standard card has room for twelve rows and eighty columns of holes. The holes are rectangular in shape. In any one column, the various combinations of one or more holes in the twelve positions can comfortably represent the digits 0 to 9, the letters of the alphabet and any other signs and symbols which may be desired, including a blank space. Thus all types of written information, which may occur in business, can be punched into cards and upon these being read into the computer, the information can be stored in the high-speed store and, if need be, transferred on to magnetic tape.

We shall now modify our computer described in Chapter 1 so that its input is a card reader instead of a paper tape reader. The input order

$$I \ n$$

now causes one number to be read from the card in the card reader and it is placed in word n of the store. The original contents of word n disappear. We supposed in Chapter 1 that all numbers can be expressed with up to ten figures. We shall now further suppose that the input order can read a word of ten letters from a card, or in fact any ten characters and place them in word n of the store. For simplicity, we shall suppose that a card has only one group of ten characters or one number punched on it, though in practice this would be wasteful of card space. We now have an input order for reading in any type of written information, once it has been punched into cards.

The output order

$$O \ n$$

now causes the number, or group of ten characters, in word n to be sent to the page printer for printing. The contents of word n remain unaltered. The page printer will print the characters in a horizontal line from left to right as they are sent to it. To cause it to start a new line or a new page, we need two new computer orders. The order

$$N \ n$$

causes the page printer to start a new line. The order

$$P \ n$$

causes the page printer to start a new page. In both these orders, the address n is irrelevant. We now have sufficient computer orders to cause the printer to print any information in any layout.

The use of magnetic tape with our computer requires the introduction of two more orders. Our computer is fitted with several magnetic tape units numbered 1, 2, 3, etc. For a particular computer run, any of these units may be fitted with reels of tape. We shall suppose a tape has only one track upon which information can be stored. Each tape will have a starting position on its track from which point the track will be divided into segments, each of which can store a number or group of ten characters.

The order

$$W1 \; n$$

causes the contents of word n of the store to be 'written' on to the next segment of the tape in tape unit number 1. The contents of word n remain unaltered but the original contents of the segment disappear. Similar orders apply for the other tape units, e.g., $W2$, $W3$.

The order

$$X1 \; n$$

causes the contents of the next segment of the tape in tape unit number 1 to be 'read' into word n of the store. The contents of the segment remain unaltered but the original contents of word n disappear.

With these new computer orders we can now proceed to consider three programs associated with payroll. In practice, programs tend to be more elaborate so as to deal with various exceptional circumstances which we have not considered. Our first program is used to set up the magnetic file of employee's basic records from punched cards. Our second program performs the payroll calculation. Finally, we shall consider the program for a cash analysis.

Before starting to consider the programs, we must define our basic record for each employee. We need eighteen words or tape segments for each record, which are as follows:

(1) payroll number
(2) surname
(3) first name or initials
(4) standard pay rate
(5) overtime pay rate
(6) first allowance

(7) second allowance
(8) third allowance
(9) total previous income, I_{m-1}
(10) total previous tax, t_{m-1}
(11) first month tax-free pay, f
(12) national insurance (employer)
(13) national insurance (employee)
(14) graduated pension scheme (employer)
(15) graduated pension scheme (employee)
(16) first voluntary deduction
(17) second voluntary deduction
(18) third voluntary deduction

In this scheme, the employee can earn either a standard
or overtime rate of pay and may be granted up to three
allowances. These pay rates and allowances are considered to be the same for every month. Segments 9 to 11
are needed for income tax information as explained in
the previous section. The national insurance contributions for employer and employee are considered to be the
same for every month. The graduated pension scheme
segments express fractions of the employee's gross pay
which go to this fund. Thus, if employer and employee
each pay 5 per cent, the segments 14 and 15 would each
contain the number 0·05. There can be up to three
voluntary deductions.

In the following three programs, we allow the special
store to contain decimals as well as whole numbers.

For our first program, we suppose that basic records
have been prepared for each employee and that these
records have been punched into cards. We suppose that
the program is punched into cards and that these are
placed in the computer's card reader followed by the
basic record cards. A reel of tape is set up on tape unit
number 1 so that the first segment is ready to be written

upon. It is upon this tape that we shall establish our magnetic file of basic records. When the computer is set going, it reads the program into words 11 to 32, then the program starts to be obeyed.

In our scheme, the payroll numbers will be the numbers 1, 2, 3, etc., in the order in which the basic records are assembled. At the end of the basic record cards, a card will be added with the number −1 punched into it. We shall see that this is used to indicate to the computer the end of the process.

The program is as shown on page 44. The first two orders read in the numbers 1 and 18 from cards at the end of the program and place them in words 1 and 2. The next two orders put zero in word 3. The reading of the basic record cards now commences. The order in word 15 causes the first card of the first record to be read into word 100. The next order writes this information on to the first segment of the tape in tape unit number 1. The next four orders add 1 to the number in word 3. Since this number was previously zero, we now have 1 in word 3. This number also remains in the accumulator. The order in word 21, causes 18 to be subtracted, giving −17. Since this is not zero, the conditional jump order in word 22 has no effect so we continue to the next order which is an unconditional jump back to word 15. This causes another card to be read into word 100 and its information is transferred to the magnetic tape. One is again added to word 3 and again we jump back to word 15. This continues until eighteen cards have been read, after which the order in word 22 causes a jump to word 24. This order causes the first card of the next record to be read. Before proceeding to read in further cards, this payroll number must be tested to see that it is positive. This test is carried out by the next three orders. If positive, the conditional jump order in word 27 causes a jump

11:*I*	1,
12:*I*	2,
13:*Z*	,
14:*R*	3,
15:*I*	100,
16:*W*1	100,
17:*Z*	,
18:*A*	3,
19:*A*	1,
20:*R*	3,
21:*S*	2,
22:*L*	24,
23:*J*	15,
24:*I*	100,
25:*Z*	,
26:*A*	100,
27:*K*	30,
28:*W*1	100,
29:*E*	,
30:*Z*	,
31:*R*	3,
32:*J*	16/
	1,
	18,

to word 30. This and the next two orders cause zero to be put in word 3 and a jump to be made to word 16. The reading of the second record then proceeds. If at word 27 the payroll number had been negative, indicating the end of the records, then we would have proceeded to word 28 which transfers this negative number to the tape to mark the end of the file. The next order stops the computer.

The list of orders in words 15 to 23 is called a *loop* because the computer obeys them repeatedly until some condition is satisfied. In this case, the condition is that all the cards of a record have been read, or more precisely, that word 3 contains the number 18.

We can now turn to our program for the payroll calculation. This is as shown on page 47. This program must be run each month to determine the pay of the employees. Information which must be provided each month consists of the number of hours each employee works at the standard rate and at the overtime rate. This information for each employee is punched into three cards: the first card has the employee's payroll number punched into it; the second card gives the number of hours he works at the standard rate and the third card gives the number of hours he works at the overtime rate. We suppose that the program is punched into cards and that these are placed in the computer's card reader followed by the sets of three cards giving the employees' hours. The basic record magnetic file is set up on tape unit number 1 and a new reel of tape is set up on tape unit number 2. This second tape will become the basic record file passing forward to next month. The computer will also print out details of the month's pay for each employee.

If we start by looking at the end of the program, we see that there are four numbers to be taken in for use with the program. The numerical value of

$$(1 - e)r$$

is needed for the income tax calculation which will be based on the simplified system described in the previous section. The last of the numbers, m, indicates the month of the financial year.

For reference in studying the program, the following words of the store will be used to hold information during the course of the calculation:

1: 1
2: 18

3: $(1 - e)r$
4: m
5: count

201 to 218: an employee's record

300: gross pay
301: pension (employer)
302: pension (employee)
303: tax-free pay, F_m
304: $I_m - F_m$
305: tax, t_m
306: tax, $t_m - t_{m-1}$
307: net pay

401: payroll number
402: standard hours
403: overtime hours

Looking now at the beginning of the program, we see four input orders to take in the four numbers at the end of program. The next two orders make word 5 contain zero. Word 5 is to contain a counting number just as word 3 did in our previous program. Words 17 to 24 contain a loop to cause the first record to be read from tape number 1 to the eighteen words starting from 201. This loop is similar to that in our previous program and only the order in word 17 requires comment. It is of the modified type and when it is obeyed, it is modified by having the contents of word 5 added to its address. Word 5 contains zero, when the loop is first entered, so the order in word 17 is obeyed as

$$X1 \quad 201.$$

Thus the first segment of tape 1 is read to word 201. The next time the order in word 17 is encountered, word 5

```
11:I        1        ,
12:I        2        ,
13:I        3        ,
14:I        4        ,
15:Z                 ,
16:R        5        ,
17:X1     201      (5), start read loop
18:Z                 ,
19:A        5        ,
20:A        1        ,
21:R        5        ,
22:S        2        ,
23:L       25        ,
24:J       17        ,
25:I      401        , input hours
26:I      402        ,
27:I      403        ,
28:Z                 , start tests
29:A      201        ,
30:S      401        ,
31:L       33        ,
32:E                 ,
33:Z                 ,
34:A      201        ,
35:K       37        ,
36:E                 ,
37:Z                 , start gross pay calculation
38:A      204        ,
39:M      402        ,
40:R      300        ,
41:Z                 ,
42:A      205        ,
43:M      403        ,
44:A      300        ,
45:A      206        ,
```

46:*A*	207	,	
47:*A*	208	,	
48:*R*	300	,	
49:*Z*		,	start pension calculation
50:*A*	300	,	
51:*M*	214	,	
52:*R*	301	,	
53:*Z*		,	
54:*A*	300	,	
55:*M*	215	,	
56:*R*	302	,	
57:*Z*		,	start tax calculation
58:*A*	300	,	
59:*A*	209	,	
60:*R*	209	,	
61:*Z*		,	
62:*A*	4	,	
63:*M*	211	,	
64:*R*	303	,	
65:*Z*		,	
66:*A*	209	,	
67:*S*	303	,	
68:*R*	304	,	
69:*Z*		,	
70:*A*	304	,	
71:*M*	3	,	
72:*R*	305	,	
73:*S*	210	,	
74:*R*	306	,	
75:*Z*		,	
76:*A*	305	,	
77:*R*	210	,	
78:*Z*		,	start net pay calculation
79:*A*	300	,	
80:*S*	306	,	

81:S	213	,	
82:S	302	,	
83:S	216	,	
84:S	217	,	
85:S	218	,	
86:R	307	,	
87:Z		,	
88:R	5	,	
89:W2	201	(5),	start write loop
90:Z		,	
91:A	5	,	
92:A	1	,	
93:R	5	,	
94:S	2	,	
95:L	97	,	
96:J	89	,	
97:P		,	start printing
98:O	201	,	
99:O	202	,	
100:O	203	,	
101:N		,	
102:O	300	,	
103:O	306	,	
104:O	307	,	
105:N		,	
106:O	301	,	
107:O	302	,	
108:J	15	/	
	1	,	
	18	,	
	$(1-e)r$	,	
	m	,	

contains 1, so the order is obeyed as

$$X1 \quad 202.$$

In this way, the segments of tape are read into the eighteen words starting at 201.

The orders in words 25 to 27 read the three cards giving the hours for the first employee and transfer the information to words 401 to 403. For our program, the sets of three cards for the employees must be arranged in the same order as the basic records. To make sure that this is so, a test is carried out in words 28 to 31. This consists of subtracting the payroll number in the set of cards from the payroll number in the basic record. If the result is not zero, the computer is stopped by the order in word 32. Otherwise we proceed to a further test to see if the payroll number is negative. If it is, the computer stops at word 36, as a negative payroll number indicates the end of the employee's records.

The calculation of the gross pay is performed by the orders in words 37 to 48. It consists of two multiplications of hours and rates of pay and the addition of the three allowances. Word 300 is used as working space as well as to hold the final result. Orders 49 to 56 calculate the amount of the employer's and employee's contribution to the graduated pension scheme. This is followed by the calculation of income tax which involves modifying words 209 and 210, being the income and tax totals passing forward to the next month. The calculation of the net pay involves merely subtracting all the deductions from the gross pay.

The orders in words 89 to 96 form a loop to write the modified basic record on to tape number 2. The construction of the loop is precisely similar to that used at the beginning of the program for reading from tape number 1.

It remains to print out the results of the pay calculation. The layout we have chosen is very wasteful of paper and involves a whole page for each employee. The page has three lines of printing: the first line gives the employee's payroll number and name; the second line gives his gross pay, income tax and net pay; the third line gives the employer's and the employee's pensions contributions. Thus the page for Sam Jones would look like this, if his payroll number is 512:

512	JONES	SAM
100.00	12.00	69.60
5.00	5.00	

At the end of the orders to effect the printing, the order in word 108 effects a jump back to the beginning of the program to cause the next record to be read from tape number 1. The whole program is a giant loop and is obeyed for each of the employee's records until the end of these records is reached, when the computer stops at word 36.

In order to keep this payroll program to a reasonable length, it has been necessary to leave out many features, the most obvious of which is the addition of the employees' payments to obtain the totals of net pay, taxes and voluntary deductions. A further feature which has been omitted is the cash analysis. Our final program indicates how this calculation is performed.

This is shown on page 52. It is in fact a fragment of program starting at word 100. Let us suppose that in word 200 we have a number representing a sum of money. Let this sum be a whole number of pounds. Our problem is to determine how many £5 and £1 notes are required to make up the sum. The method is to subtract 5 from the sum repeatedly until a negative number is obtained, at the same time counting how many 5's are subtracted.

```
100:Z          ,
101:R         1,
102:R       401,
103:R       402,
104:Z          ,
105:A       200,
106:S       301,
107:K       109,
108:J       115,
109:R       200,
110:Z          ,
111:A         1,
112:A       302,
113:R         1,
114:J       104,
115:Z          ,
116:A         1,
117:R       401,
118:Z          ,
119:R         1,
120:Z          ,
121:A       200,
122:S       302,
123:K       125,
124:J       131,
125:R       200,
126:Z          ,
127:A         1,
128:A       302,
129:R         1,
130:J       120,
131:Z          ,
132:A         1,
133:R       402,
134:E          ,
```

The negative number then has 5 added to it and 1's are subtracted in the same way. We require the number of £5 notes to be placed in word 401 and the number of £1 notes to be placed in word 402. We suppose the numbers 5 and 1 are stored in words 301 and 302.

The first four orders of the program put zero in words 1, 401 and 402. We then subtract 5 from the number in word 200 and test that the result is positive with the order in word 107. The orders in words 109 to 114 put the result back in word 200 and 1 is added to word 1, which is used for counting the 5's. When the negative result is obtained, the order in word 108 causes a jump to word 115. At this point, word 1 contains the required number of £5 notes and it remains to transfer this number to word 401. Words 115 to 117 contain orders for this. The orders in words 118 and 119 put zero in word 1 ready to start counting the £1 notes. The next fourteen orders are precisely similar to those for counting the £5 notes, but 1 is subtracted each time round the loop instead of 5. Finally the computer stops at word 134. By adding further counting loops, it would be possible to determine the coins required for sums involving fractional parts of a pound. By including this fragment of program in the payroll calculation, it would be possible to determine the total numbers of notes and coins required for all the wage payments.

3   Stores and Accounting

The business world, at least in so far as private enterprise is concerned, may be regarded as made up of *companies*. The dealings of the business world consist of the transfer of goods and services, in exchange for money, between one company and another or between a company and individual members of the public.

In addition to the word 'company', the expressions 'firm', 'business organization' and 'business concern' are in use and have the same meaning.

Company Activities

Companies can be small, as in the case of a person who owns and runs his business without employing any other labour, or they can be extremely large international organizations. But whatever the size of the organization, there are certain features which are common to most, if not all, companies. It is this fact which has enabled governments to introduce laws to ensure the proper conduct of company affairs.

A company usually needs to occupy premises for the conduct of its business. These premises may be owned by or leased to the company. The company will usually hire labour and employ the services of professional consultants such as accountants, solicitors and technical experts. While some companies are concerned entirely with offering a service, such as groups of solicitors or doctors, the great mass of business activity is concerned with the processing and distribution of material products, many of which will eventually be bought by the public.

Companies which deal with material products (collectively referred to as *goods*) will, in general, have two or more distinct areas of activity. The first of these is the *purchase* of materials from other companies, without which the work of the company would grind to a halt. An exception to this is the self-sufficient peasant farmer who farms his own land. Another exception could be a company which extracts raw materials from its own land but usually such a company would need to purchase equipment for use in its operations.

The second area of activity is the *sale* of the company's products. This activity is essential to the continued existence of the company. The only exception is again the self-sufficient farmer, but very few farmers indeed choose such a degree of isolation. The sales area is, of course, equally important to companies not involved with material products.

The third area of activity is the *storage* of material items. Such storage is necessary for purchased material while it is waiting to be processed by the company in its own factories. It is necessary for the company's finished products, while they are waiting to be sold. It may also be necessary as an intermediate stage in the production process, as for example in the maturing of wines. Storage may in fact be the sole activity of a company, e.g., the storage of furniture. While most objects can be stored by standing them on the floor or on shelves, some products require special storage arrangements such as refrigeration for perishable foodstuffs, silos for flour and special containers for corrosive chemicals. The material products in storage at a particular time are often referred to as *stock*.

The fourth area of activity is the processing of purchased materials to produce the products of the company.

c

Such processing may be completely chemical in nature or it may involve various processes of manufacture and assembly with the need for differing degrees of manual effort, mechanization and automation. This area of activity is summed up in the word *production*.

Our fifth area groups together the activities involved in disposing of the company's products after a sale has been effected. These include the packaging and transport or mailing of the product and after sales service.

Finally, as a miscellaneous group we must add activities which, although not directly touching upon the movement of materials through the company's premises, are none-theless important to the future progress of the company. These activities include market research and advertising, research laboratories for the development of new pro-ducts and the improvement of existing ones, a personnel department concerned with training schemes, catering and welfare facilities, and by no means least the office and accounting department.

Physical and Financial Aspects

The first five areas of activity, which we may regard as the main activities of the company, have a physical aspect in the movement of materials from reception through pro-cessing and storage to final dispatch. Each of these activ-ities, however, also has its financial aspect because every phase of the physical activity costs money and the com-pany is interested in making each phase as efficient as current techniques will permit.

It follows that, from the point of view of management, the proper running of the company involves keeping a close watch on both the physical processes going on in the company and the costs involved in them. It is vital to the survival of the company that total receipts of money from sales should not fall below the total costs of running the company.

Computer Applications

Computers have found application in all six areas of company activity in both their physical and financial aspects.

An interesting application in the personnel department is the preparation of an internal telephone directory for the company. This is done by adding the employee's telephone number to his basic pay record. It then requires only a short program to print out a list of names and telephone numbers which can then be photographically copied for printing. Any change in an employee's telephone number is conveyed to the record file at the same time as the payroll amendments. An up-to-date telephone directory can be obtained at any time by running the computer program.

Computers are extensively used in the research departments of companies for the scientific calculations associated with the design and development of new products.

Computer applications in the production and distribution areas will be discussed in the next chapter. Here we shall consider how a computer can be applied in the first three areas of activity. Before doing so, however, we must look more closely at the procedures involved.

In all dealings between companies or between a company and a private citizen, the concept of an *account* is basic. We might imagine that an account is a money box. A particular company has such a box for each company or citizen with which it has dealings. At any instant of time, a box may contain an amount of money which can be positive or negative. Let us suppose company *A* takes on dealings with a new customer *B*. When it is agreed that dealings are to commence, company A creates a box for B which is initially empty. If now, B makes a payment of £100 to the company for goods to be ordered later, this £100 goes in his box. When B subsequently orders £50 worth of goods from A, the goods are delivered and £50 is removed from B's box and transferred to the funds of the company. Later, when B orders a further £75 worth of goods, the goods are again delivered and the sum of £75 is removed from B's box to the funds of the company, leaving $-$£25 in B's box. B then makes a payment to the company of £30 so that his box now contains £5. Matters continue like this as long as dealings last. Some customers prefer to 'settle' their accounts immediately, i.e., make the box contain zero, whereas others are continually lagging in their payments.

In practice, the keeping of separate money boxes for each customer is most inconvenient and so instead a card is kept upon which the sum of money is written. Incoming money then goes into one big box and it is only necessary to check periodically that the total influx of money corresponds to the changes in the amounts written on the account cards. In its simplest form, the account card has on it, the customer's name and the latest value of the sum of money in the account. Often, further information is also listed: the customer's address, details of recent dealings and details of price reductions with which the customer may be privileged. Another item of information which is mentioned is the maximum extent of the *credit* which the customer is allowed. This is the extent to which his account is allowed to go negative. If the customer makes an order which would cause his account to go more negative than the stated amount, the order must be refused and delivery does not take place.

If B orders goods from company A, so as to make B's account negative, then from B's point of view the account is an *account payable* and from *A*'s point of view it is an *account receivable*.

If *B* wishes to obtain goods from *A* without immediate payment, a *hire purchase* agreement may be entered into under which repayment is made in stages over a period of time. Hire purchase accounting is thus somewhat more involved and details of the agreement must be recorded. An American development of hire purchase is known as *revolving credit*. Under this arrangement, the customer's credit limit is decided at the beginning, say £60. The agreement fixes the repayment amount at say £10 per month. The customer need not spend immediately to the full limit of his credit and is free to make further purchases later, provided that the credit limit is at no time exceeded. For example, suppose the initial purchase is £40. After two monthly repayments, the debt is reduced to £20. The customer can now make a further purchase of up to £40. Unlike a hire purchase agreement which is repaid after a specified amount of time, a revolving credit goes on indefinitely. The widespread use of revolving credit has had to await the computer, owing to the complicated nature of the accounting.

The account concept finds an application within the company. It is convenient to create accounts to cover costs arising within the company's activities although no money actually passes in or out of the company. For example, the cost of oiling machinery could be an account, although the oil would in fact be obtained from the company store. It is true, of course, that the oil had to be purchased from another company in the first place, but this purchase would appear in the ordinary outside accounts. The manipulation of these internal accounts is called *cost accounting* and it is most important in large companies where the cost of producing a particular product must be accurately worked out. Only in this way can the company be sure that continued production of the product is worthwhile in the face of competition from other firms.

The accounting we have so far considered has involved the recording of sums of money. Record cards are used in a similar manner to hold information about the company's storage arrangements. In this case, a record is concerned with the number of a particular product at present in storage. In addition to this information, the record must also state the minimum level to which this number shall be allowed to fall before a further supply is ordered. The normal size of this replacement order is also recorded. Other necessary information is the cost price and selling price of the product and the purchase tax on it.

The interaction between these different accounts depends on the type of business and many variations are possible. For example, a wholesale warehouse employs salesmen to visit retail shops to collect orders. The salesman writes out the order in triplicate. The order form consists of a space for the name of the retail shop and space for the name of each product and the number required. The order, in triplicate, is sent to the warehouse for immediate action. The goods are dispatched and one copy of the order is sent with them as a *delivery note*. This enables the goods to be checked upon arrival at the retail shop. The second copy of the order remains in the warehouse in case dispute subsequently arises. The third copy goes to the office so that the account of the shop can be adjusted. At frequent intervals, an *invoice* is sent from the office to the shop. This is a statement of the amount of money owing. The office copy of the order then passes to the stores accounting section, where the records of items in stock are adjusted and from where replacement orders are initiated. It will be apparent that the delivery note and the invoice contain essentially the same information and some firms send only the one document. The invoice can however also give details of outstanding debts remaining to be paid.

In the above procedure, it will be seen that due to errors, breakages and pilferage, the actual stock levels will not usually agree exactly with those stated in the records. For this reason, a check on stocks must be made from time to time. All items need not be checked at the same time, however, and the work can be spread over the year and undertaken in relatively slack periods.

In considering the application of computers to these procedures, we must remember that electromechanical accounting machines were already well established on the scene and they have not yielded readily to the challenge of the computer. This has also been true to some extent in the case of payroll, but the ever increasing complication of the tax calculations has enabled the computer to establish itself more readily in that field. In most branches of accounting, the calculation is limited to the addition and subtraction of figures with the occasional multiplication and possibly the evaluation of percentages. Such calculations are well within the limits of most accounting machines.

In the previous chapter we saw how a magnetic file can be set up for the basic records of the employees of a company by first punching them into cards and using a computer program to transfer the information on to magnetic tape. In the same way stores records and accounts can be set up as magnetic files. These files can then be used in connection with further programs in order to maintain the files up to date and to produce printed output in the form of invoices and stores replacement orders. We shall consider a specific example in more detail in the following section.

During the running of payroll and invoice programs

it is usual to have an extra reel of magnetic tape on the computer upon which can be stored items of information which are significant to the overall finances of the company. Such items might be weekly wages totals for different departments, tax totals and weekly sales in different ranges of products. From time to time, such 'summary tapes' are used with a program for calculating the overall financial position. The output from the computer consists of a series of *management reports* which are tables setting out facts about the company's performance. It is important that the correct facts should be presented and in a concise form. Properly presented information enables the managers of the various departments to see at a glance if performance is falling below expectation. The cause of any inefficiency can then be investigated before it causes an appreciable loss to the company. This principle of underlining low performance and difficulties is known as *management by exception*. As long as things are running smoothly there is little for the manager to do, but as soon as things start to go wrong, he has his hands full. It is thus a valuable aid to the manager, if the computer can be programmed to produce reports which indicate clearly any difficulty within the organization.

Two management reports which are traditionally produced to indicate the state of a company's finances are the *income statement* and the *balance sheet*. Prior to the computer era, these reports were produced at the end of the financial year with much hectic effort on the part of clerical and accounting staff. With the summary tapes maintaining up-to-date information on company affairs, it requires little effort to run the program which produces these two reports. The result is that they can be produced every month instead of annually and consequently give extra information, such as seasonal performance. Also, overall trends in company affairs can be more readily discerned and at an earlier stage.

The income statement indicates the company's performance over a period of time, whereas the balance sheet is a financial snapshot of the company, taken at a particular instant of time. Traditionally, the period of time was the financial year and the instant of time was the end of the financial year.

A computer-produced income statement should indicate performance for the month just ended and for the year-to-date. Reporting the information in this manner enables the performance to be seen in the most recent period as well as over a longer period, so that a trend can be established.

The basic financial equation for any type of business is

$$p = s - c$$

where p is the *profit*, s is the value of total sales and c is value of total costs and expenses. Although some businesses may operate for limited periods without making a profit, it is essential for the survival of a company that there should be at least some profit over a longer period. The simplest type of income statement consists of a statement of the values of s, c and p for the period. Normally, however, the sales and costs will be itemized in some detail. More particularly in retail businesses, it is usual to separate costs into two types, namely *costs of goods sold* and *operating expenses*. The *gross margin of profit* is obtained by subtracting the costs of goods sold from the total sales. The profit is obtained by subtracting the operating expenses from the gross margin of profit. This procedure provides an important indicator of where profits are coming from.

Suppose that a businessman is dissatisfied with his level of profits. By examining performance in companies similar to his own, he finds that other companies have about the same level of expenses. On the other hand, he finds that his gross margin of profit is lower than what is typically the case. He further looks at his costs of goods sold and finds they are in line with similar companies. This provides him with a perspective with which to examine his sales. It is possible that his prices are too low on certain lines, causing him to lose adequate gross margin where it is important. On the other hand, it could be the reverse, in that prices on certain items are too high, causing him to lose important sales volume on these lines. This example has been included to show how important the income statement is to a company; to emphasize that it is far more than a historical record. This report is a vital tool with which to determine corrective action and profit planning. This is why a system, which provides an accurate up-to-date income statement each month, is so important.

The extra details, normally included in an income statement, are important and must be scrutinized even if the profit level is satisfactory. One reason is that there may be items in either sales or expense which are peculiar to this period and without which the profit for this period would be far different. An unusually large sale to an institution or a non-recurring drop in sales, such as would be caused by a blizzard, are examples. Another reason is that there may be an unsatisfactory condition or trend which will not affect net profit this period but which will reduce profits later. An example of this would be an excessive build up in stocks in relation to sales. This could necessitate an excessive markdown in prices later, which would reduce profits considerably.

Operating expenses must also be scrutinized but it is wrong to take the view that all expenses are bad and should be reduced. The object of the company is to make the best profit. It may be that an increase in certain expenses, such as lighting to make a shop more attractive, might substantially increase the volume of sales, and, as a result, increase the net profit. Careful records of expenses and trends provide the basis for expense budgeting. By having accurate, computer-produced data on each type of expense and its relative percentage to sales, it is possible to plan expense outlays in advance, on the basis of anticipated sales.

The balance sheet is a statement of the company's *assets* and *liabilities* at a particular instant of time. Assets are what the company owns. Liabilities are what the company owes. Assets are those items of wealth which the company needs in order to be in business. If you are a manufacturer, your assets probably include your buildings, machinery and stocks of raw materials. In wholesaling or retailing, one of the most important assets is always the stock of goods for sale. In many businesses, another important asset is accounts receivable, because it is customary in many lines of trade to sell a considerable amount of goods on credit. This means, of course, that instead of receiving cash, another asset item, the company receives a customer's promise to pay at a later date. Since this becomes a legal obligation by the customer, such accounts receivable are regarded as assets. Liabilities are the financial obligations of the company to others. Accounts payable are usually important liabilities because a large amount of goods are purchased from suppliers on some type of trade credit. The excess of the company's assets over its liabilities is the company's *net worth*, i.e., what it would be worth if regarded as an item of wealth.

The balance sheet, and the financial picture it presents, may not seem significant at first sight. However, specific items and trends may indicate future profits or losses or serious financial problems which could be developing in the company. These may not yet be apparent by an examination of the income statement alone. The balance sheet is also of value to bankers and credit managers who use it to evaluate the financial status of the company for credit purposes.

The two management reports we have considered are backed up by others giving more details of particular aspects or divisions of the company.

In certain types of retail business it is possible to record sales automatically by connecting the cash register to a paper tape punch. In this way, sales data are ready for immediate input to the computer without the costly preliminary of punching into cards. Another technique is to attach cardboard tags to the goods by means of threads. The tags have holes punched in them which identify the items. When the goods are sold, the tags are removed by the shop assistants, then, by means of an appropriate reader, the information can be read from the tags into a computer. These methods have enabled the advantages of computer processing to be extended to quite small retail undertakings. If, further, the shop assistants are each allocated a number which can be punched with the sale, then the computer can prepare a *salesperson's productivity report* showing the number and the total cash value of the sales effected by each assistant. Payroll is a substantial part of a company's expenses; in some types of business it exceeds the total of all other expenses combined. This report enables the manager to compare the overall performance with prior periods and with similar companies. It also provides a yardstick to measure the individual assistant's performance. A productivity report can similarly be produced for salesmen who send in orders to a warehouse. Poor performance may not be the fault of the assistant, but the report at any rate draws attention to the matter which can then be investigated.

The application of computers to the areas of company activity considered in this section enables information on these areas to be systematically maintained in an up-to-date condition and is such that reports can be produced at short notice, no matter how farflung or complex the organization may be. The computer and its reports are aids to better management but are not substitutes for management. They will not take the place of front-line operating experience. They will, however, provide information which can be used in the light of that experience. This is scientific management, supported by computer-produced information. The optimum profit picture of which the company is capable should be the result.

Computer Scheme

In this section we shall consider in a little more detail how a computer can be applied to the office work associated with the wholesale warehouse mentioned in the previous section. We shall consider the computer to be limited to four magnetic tape units.

The purpose of our scheme is to maintain records of stock and customer accounts. The computer responds to customers' orders by issuing an invoice and correcting recorded stock levels. If necessary a replacement order note is printed. The computer responds to delivery notes of stocks received from suppliers by correcting recorded stock levels.

Our scheme involves the use of three files, namely, the stock file, the customer file and the outstanding orders file. We shall suppose for simplicity that these files can each be contained on one reel of magnetic tape. In the various computer runs, tapes will be required for the old and new versions of these files. In addition, four further reels of tape will be required and will be referred to as reels *A*, *B*, *C*, and *D*.

Programs must be written which are used to establish the files initially from information punched into cards. Other programs must be available to modify the files to cover such eventualities as the introduction of new customers, changes of customers' addresses, the payment of money by customers and increases in prices. These programs are no more complicated than the payroll programs and will not be considered further.

The stock file consists of records, each of fifteen words. The end of the records is marked by a −1 as in the payroll example. This applies also to the two other files. The fifteen words are as follows:

(1) commodity number
(2) commodity name
(3) number of items in store
(4) reorder level
(5) reorder quantity
(6) cost price per item
(7) purchase tax per item
(8) sale price per item
(9), (10) name of supplier
(11) to (15) address of supplier

Each commodity is given a distinct number and name and the records in the stock file are arranged in ascending order of commodity number. A commodity is to be reordered when stocks fall to the level given by (4) and the number of items in this replacement order is given by (5). The sale price of the item will normally exceed the sum of the cost price plus purchase tax. The excess is the gross profit margin on the item. The record ends with two words for the supplier's name and five for his address. The five address words could be one for street number, two for name of street, one for town and one for county. As an example, kettles have commodity number 97. There are 1500 kettles in the store. When stocks fall to 500 kettles a replacement order of 1000 must be made. The cost price of a kettle, i.e., what the supplier charges, is £0·75. Purchase tax is £0·25 and the sale price is £1·50. The supplier is Hardware Deliveries of 15 Works Crescent, Blacktown, Smogshire.

The customer file consists of records, each of ten words which are as follows:

(1) customer number
(2), (3) name of customer
(4) to (8) address of customer
(9) amount of account
(10) credit limit

Each customer is given a distinct customer number and the records in the customer file are arranged in ascending order of customer number.

New orders from customers are punched into cards. Up to 21 cards may be needed for an order. The first card is punched with the customer number. Subsequent pairs of cards are punched with a commodity number and a number indicating the quantity required. The order can cover up to ten commodities. If the order actually involves more than ten commodities, then it must be broken into two or more separate orders. If the order involves less than ten commodities, the order can be terminated with a card punched with the number −1. Thus if kettles have commodity number 97 and pans have commodity number 98 then the order

518
97
3
98

2
−1

would indicate to the computer that customer 518 has ordered three kettles and two pans. This same pattern is used in the records of the outstanding orders file. This file is a list of customers' orders which have not been satisfied due to items being out of stock.

Delivery notes indicating the arrival of goods at the warehouse from suppliers are also punched into cards. The method of representation is exactly the same as for orders except that the first card is punched with the number −2. The computer can be made to distinguish this number from the positive customer numbers by means of a conditional jump. Hence the computer is enabled to deal with orders and delivery notes in different ways.

Having specified all the records and input data, we are now in a position to consider the computer runs necessary to process the warehouse office work. While a computer could be used with the scheme described in the previous section, we shall in fact introduce some minor modifications. The salesman now sends in only one copy of the order and he sends it directly to the office. The computer produces an invoice which then goes to the warehouse so that the goods can be dispatched. The invoice is sent with the goods and so acts as a delivery note. In the case of goods received into the warehouse, the goods are put away then the delivery note for them is sent to the office from the warehouse. Thus, during the course of a typical working day, orders and delivery notes will be arriving steadily. Upon arrival, the information they contain is punched into cards and these are held until the next day's session on the computer. The computer session to deal with the work requires six runs.

In run 1, the outstanding orders file is fitted on one tape unit and tape A is fitted on another. Yesterday's accumulation of cards is placed in the card reader. The program for this run has the effect of reading in the information from the cards and transferring it to tape A but in a slightly different form. Each record on tape A consists of only three segments:

(1) customer number
(2) commodity number
(3) quantity ordered

Thus, an order involving five commodities would be transformed into five of these records on tape A. Delivery notes are similarly transformed except that -2 goes into the customer number segment of each record on tape A. This enables deliveries to be distinguished from orders in later runs. When all the cards have been read and transferred on to tape A in this manner, the information in the outstanding orders file is similarly transferred to tape A. Thus, at the end of the run, all new information and outstanding orders are on tape A in the simplified layout. Both tapes are rewound and tape A passes forward to run 2.

In run 2, the information on tape A is *sorted* and transferred to tape B. This sorting involves altering the sequence of the records so that they are arranged in ascending commodity number. The technique of sorting will be described in the final section of this chapter.

In run 3 the stock file is brought up to date. The old and new versions of this are set on two of the tape units and tape B is set on another. Tape C is set on the remaining tape unit. This tape is to receive the orders from tape B but in an extended form. The program for this run causes tape B to be read and each record is dealt with as will now be described. First the customer number is examined to see if it is positive (using a K order). If not, then the record relates to a delivery and the stock file is advanced (i.e., the information is passed unchanged from the old tape to the new) until the record is found having the same commodity number as that of the delivery. This record is then corrected by adding the quantity delivered to the quantity in stock. On the other hand, if the customer number is positive, then the record from tape B relates to an order. The stock file is advanced until the record is found having the same commodity number as that of the order. The quantity of the order is subtracted from the quantity in stock and the result is tested with a K order. If the result is negative, the order cannot be satisfied because the stock is inadequate. If the result is positive (or zero), the order can be satisfied. In this case the result of the subtraction becomes the new quantity in stock. Whether the order can be satisfied or not, it is transferred to tape C in an extended form. The record on tape C consists of eight segments made up of the three used in the records on tapes A and B, together with

(4) commodity name
(5) cost price of order
(6) purchase tax on order
(7) sale price of order
(8) 1 for satisfied; -1 for unsatisfied

Of this information, (4) is copied from the stock file. The values (5) to (7) are obtained by multiplying the order quantity by the money per item as stated in segments (6) to (8) of the stock file. Finally (8) is given the value 1 if the order is satisfied and -1 if it is not. Deliveries as well as orders are transferred to tape C, but the extensions (4) to (8) are in this case left blank.

If the order is satisfied it is necessary to test further to see if the satisfying of the order has caused the quantity in stock to fall below the reorder level. This will be the case if the old quantity in stock was above the reorder level and the new quantity in stock is below the reorder level. In this case, the computer prints out a replacement order. This states the name and address of the supplier, the commodity name and the reorder quantity, all of which are obtained from the commodity record in the stock file.

At the end of run 3, the extended orders have been transferred to tape C and all necessary replacement orders have been printed on paper bearing the company's own name and address. These orders can be posted immediately in window envelopes.

In run 4, two reels of tape are set on the tape units. They are tape C and the new version of the unsatisfied orders file. Also a summary tape can be used in this run to record essential details of the day's activities. The program transfers unsatisfied orders from tape C to the unsatisfied orders file, in a form suitable for input in run 1, and the essential details (e.g., total costs, total sales, total purchase tax) to the summary tape.

In run 5, the information on tape C is sorted and transferred to tape D. This sorting involves altering the sequence of the records so that they are arranged in ascending customer number.

In run 6, invoices are produced and the customers' accounts are adjusted. Tape D and the old and new versions of the customer file are set on the tape units. As a result of the sort in run 5, the customers' orders have now effectively been reassembled, because the day's orders for a particular customer will have been grouped together on tape D. The program for run 6 causes each customer's order to be dealt with as will now be described. The customer file is advanced until the customer's record is found. From this, the customer's name and address are printed out; also the value of his account prior to the

present order. For each commodity in the present order
the following information is printed: commodity number,
commodity name, quantity ordered, sale price. If the
order for this commodity cannot be satisfied, the sale
price is left out. This indicates the position to the customer. When all commodities in the customer's order
have been printed, the total of the prices is calculated and
is also printed on the invoice. This total is also used to
correct the customer's record in the customer file: the
total is subtracted from the account value held in word
(9) of the customer's record. It is now necessary to check
that the customer's credit limit has not been exceeded. If it
has, a remark to this effect is printed at the bottom of the
invoice. At the end of run 6, the new version of the
customer file is put away and the printed invoices are sent
to the warehouse for dispatch with the goods. In the
warehouse, any invoices which have exceeded credit
limits are sent to the manager for a decision. The manager
may allow the goods to go. If he decides not to let them
go, the stock levels recorded in the stock file must be
adjusted at the next computer session, since they have
been recorded as if the goods were to be sent. The information on tapes A to D is no longer required and so these
tapes can be used again the next day.

This completes the computer session for the warehouse
office work. In view of the essentially simple nature of the
operations involved, it may surprise the reader that six
runs on the computer are required whereas our more
complicated payroll calculation was performed in one
run. The extra difficulty arises from the need to interrelate
information from two files, namely, the customer and
stock files. In payroll, the only file was of the employees'
basic pay records. The search of the two files is facilitated
by the sorting in runs 2 and 5. Without this preliminary
sorting, the search would involve the backward and

forward movement of the tapes which would be prohibitively time consuming.

Sorting

The sorting of information is best carried out before it is put into a computer. For example, machinery exists for efficiently sorting punched cards and so such cards can be put in proper order before being used as input to the computer. However, we saw in the previous section that situations can arise in which it is necessary to sort inside the computer. For even if we had put the input cards in commodity order before input to the computer, the problem of sorting to customer order would have remained.

In this section we shall consider a computer method for sorting information held on a magnetic tape. It is supposed that the information is made up of records each of a fixed number of segments and a particular segment in each record holds a number which will identify the record (e.g., commodity number or customer number). Our problem is to rearrange the records so that their identification numbers are in ascending order.

The method is known as *merge sorting*. It requires four reels of magnetic tape P, Q, R and S and we shall suppose tape P holds the information initially. The tapes are regarded as in pairs P,Q and R,S. Tape Q must initially hold no record. The program for merge sorting causes tapes P and Q to be read. The records are merged together then separated into two groups which are transferred to tapes R and S. The rules for merging and separating will be explained below. When all the records have passed to tapes R and S this first phase of the process is complete. In the second phase, the records on tapes R and S are read, merged and separated to tapes P and Q. In the third phase, the records on tapes P and Q

are read, merged and separated to tapes R and S. The process continues until all the records end up on one tape, when they will also be in ascending order.

We must now look more closely at the read, merge and separate procedure. Let us consider the situation when tapes P and Q are being read. At any instant of time, there will be a record just read from P. Let this have identification number p. There will also be a record just read from Q. Let this have identification number q. The object of the procedure is to build up a group of records on tape R in ascending order, as far as possible. Let r be the identification number of the record just transferred to tape R. We examine if the smaller of p and q is greater than r. If so, then the corresponding record can be transferred to tape R and the next record read from P or Q. If not, then we examine if the larger of p and q is greater than r. If so, then the corresponding record can be transferred to tape R and the next record read from P or Q. On the other hand, if r is greater than both p and q, then the ascending sequence on tape R cannot be continued. In this case we start building a new sequence on tape S starting with the smaller of p and q.

To illustrate all this, let us suppose to start that tape P has eight records on it, with identification numbers 1 to 8. Suppose initially these are in the order

$$7 \ 5 \ 1 \ 8 \ 2 \ 6 \ 3 \ 4$$

where record 7 is at the beginning of the tape and record 4 is at the end. Tape Q is empty so, during the first phase, records can be read from tape P only. The first is record 7 which goes to tape R. The next is record 5. Since 7 is greater than 5, an increasing sequence cannot be continued on tape R so this record goes to tape S and we endeavour to continue an increasing sequence on this tape. Unfortunately 5 is greater than 1, so such a se-

quence cannot be continued; instead record 1 goes to
tape R. The next record, 8, can also go to R because 8 is
greater than 1. This sequence cannot be continued any
further as 2 is less than 8. Continuing in this fashion, we
end up with records on the tapes as follows:

$$R: 7\ 1\ 8\ 3\ 4$$
$$S: 5\ 2\ 6$$

In the second phase, records 5 and 7 are the first to be
considered. Since 5 is the lesser, this record goes to tape
P. Record 2 can now be read from tape S and we have,
for the first time, three numbers 5, 7 and 2 to be compared.
Since 2 is less than 5, this record cannot continue the
sequence on tape P. But 7 is greater than 5 so record 7
can continue the sequence on P and record 1 is read from
R. We now compare 7, 1 and 2. It is not possible to
continue the sequence any further so we begin again on
tape Q. At the end of the second phase, the records are
held as follows:

$$P: 5\ 7\ 3\ 4$$
$$Q: 1\ 2\ 6\ 8$$

The third phase gives:

$$R: 1\ 2\ 5\ 6\ 7\ 8$$
$$S: 3\ 4$$

and the fourth phase gives:

$$P: 1\ 2\ 3\ 4\ 5\ 6\ 7\ 8$$
$$Q:$$

In order for merge sorting to work, it is not necessary
for the identification numbers to be a consecutive sequence. Also it is possible for different records to have the
same identification number. Finally, as a further example,
let us consider an initial sequence

$$P: 9\ 2\ 7\ 1\ 7\ 4\ 7$$

The first phase gives:

R: 9 1 7
S: 2 7 4 7

The second phase gives:

P: 2 7 9
Q: 1 4 7 7

The third phase gives the ordered sequence:

P: 1 2 4 7 7 7 9
Q:

4 Production and Distribution

We now turn to the actual production processes which a company undertakes in order to convert the materials purchased from suppliers into the company's finished products.

In some types of production, where the end product is a traditional item and where the same item is turned out year after year, there is little need for clerical activity. For each 1000 items produced, the amount of raw material is a known quantity. The rate of production is known and so the whole process can proceed smoothly from start to finish. Examples of this type of production are popular foodstuffs, such as cornflakes and baked beans.

At the other extreme is the production of one single item, usually of a large and complex construction. The planning problem for this type of work will be considered in Chapter 11.

Here we are concerned with the intermediate type of production, where a number of standard items are being made, but where the production process is not the smooth flow of materials which we first considered. This intermediate type of work is found extensively in the construction industry, particularly in the manufacture and assembly of metal parts. Aircraft production is an example. This type of endeavour gives rise to extensive clerical work in planning and directing the various stages of construction and in seeing that materials and components are available at the right times and places.

As a specific example, an Italian firm produces small-scale switch gear, electric plugs, ducting for power supplies and a variety of associated electrical equipment. It supplies 75 per cent of the Italian market and has substantial export sales. Daily the factory handles 600,000 items of equipment. The firm makes 3500 different end products from 18,000 basic parts. It needs 400 suppliers for its materials and its products go out to 500 wholesalers. This firm has bought a computer to aid in effective and efficient control of the firm's manufacturing activities.

This example indicates the scale of the task and the case for computer processing of the information would seem to be clearly established. This area of company activity has, however, been very resistant to computer methods, particularly in Britain. A possible explanation is that the computer schemes so far devised are not sufficiently flexible to deal with the variety of situations which can arise in the medium-sized factories which make up so much of British industry.

Production Control

Before we can appreciate how the computer is applied to production control we must look more closely at what is involved in this control, whether it is undertaken by computer or by traditional human methods.

It must also be mentioned at this stage that we shall not be concerned with the increasing number of applications where a computer is linked directly to the manufacturing processes. This is *automation* and a detailed study of it is beyond the scope of this book.

Let us consider the production programme for a factory extending over a financial year. For simplicity we shall suppose that a clean start is made at the beginning of the year and that all previous work is out of the way. Some months before the year begins, the production managers will have been planning the activities of the factory, at least in outline. Some companies base their production programmes on definite orders received from customers. Others base their programmes on anticipated sales, which are estimated from current sales trends. Whichever method is used, a plan is drawn up which states the intended production of each of the company's products and the dates upon which batches of the various products will be ready for delivery.

The next step in the planning is to break down or 'explode' each product into its component parts in order that the total requirements of parts can be assessed. It is convenient to think of a finished product as made up of assemblies, sub-assemblies and parts. A *part* is the lowest level of item used in the work of assembly. Parts are put together to form *sub-assemblies*. Parts and sub-assemblies are put together to form *assemblies*. Finally, parts, sub-assemblies and assemblies are put together to form a finished product. In the case of aircraft production, an aircraft is the finished product. The airframe and the engines can be regarded as assemblies. Of the airframe, the wings and tail section can be regarded as sub-assemblies. In this scheme, there are thus four levels of complexity from parts to finished products. It may be convenient to have more levels for some types of assembly work.

In order to calculate the total number of the various parts needed for a production programme, the *bill of material* is consulted for each finished product. This is a list of the assemblies, sub-assemblies and parts required. Bills of material are maintained not only for finished products but also for assemblies and sub-assemblies. Thus the assemblies in a given finished product can be broken down into sub-assemblies which in turn can be broken down into parts.

To take a simple illustration: The bill of material for product *A* indicates that it is made up of two assemblies *B*, four sub-assemblies *C* and parts *d* and *e*. On consulting the bill of material for *B*, we find it is made up of three sub-assemblies *C*, two parts *a* and one part *b*. Sub-assembly *C* is made up of six parts *a*, one part *b* and one part *c*. Thus, *A* breaks down to

$$2B \ 4C \ d \ e$$

and breaking down the *B*'s gives

$$4a \ 2b \ 10C \ d \ e$$

and breaking down the *C*'s gives

$$64a \ 12b \ 10c \ d \ e.$$

A realistic example would be quite tedious to follow but this arithmetic could readily be transferred to a computer.

In addition to calculating the number of parts required, the dates when they are needed to fit into the production programme must also be determined. This can be done if the bill of material indicates the requirements and the number of weeks before completion that these requirements are needed. Thus, for product *A* above, the assemblies *B* and parts *d* and *e* are required two weeks before the completion date for the product *A* and the sub-assemblies *C* are required one week before. As a result of the combined calculations, a time table can be prepared indicating the various parts required during each week of the year.

The basic parts of which the more complex assemblies are made up fall into two categories: those bought from suppliers and those manufactured within the company's factory. For parts bought outside, the company stores must be informed of requirements so that orders can be placed in plenty of time. The requirements for manufactured parts determines the manufacturing programme for the year. This manufacturing will give rise to the need for raw materials so the stores are again involved.

The manufacturing work of the company is undertaken in one or more workshops where machines of various types are installed. As with assembly, the manufacturing processes require time for their execution. This time is made up of time for movement of work from one machine to another, machine setting up time and time for the machining of each part. We might consider as an example the manufacture of gear wheels in three stages. The raw material is a rod of metal of circular cross-section. One machine cuts the rod into short lengths to form the wheels. A second machine cuts out the teeth and a third machine smooths the edges of each wheel. This type of production usually involves 'batching'. This means that production is only undertaken for fairly large batches at a time, it being uneconomical to set up the machines to produce only a few parts.

From the year's timetable of requirements for manufactured parts, the production manager determines the amount of work required of the machines, on the assumption that parts are not made until they are required. This amount of work is the *machine loading* and it is calculated for each type of machine and each week of the year. Some weeks may be slack periods while in other weeks machines are overloaded. Overloading can be dealt with by overtime working or by arranging for some of the parts to be made by another firm. This latter solution must be resorted to with caution, however, as no control can be exerted over the activities of the other firm and non-delivery of parts could seriously hold up assembly work. If overloading cannot be dealt with in either of these ways it is necessary to manufacture some of the parts ahead of requirements and to hold them in store until needed. This rephasing of the manufacturing work, called *work scheduling*, is performed in order to obtain satisfactory machine loading. Similar work scheduling is required on the assembly side of the factory to ensure that adequate space and labour are available.

When the work schedule is satisfactory, *works documentation* can commence. This is the preparation of detailed instructions to various parts of the factory regarding the stages of the work. These instructions fall into three main sections. *Material requisitions* indicate to the stores, where and when materials are to be sent to feed the machines. *Route sheets* indicate the route followed by items between machines in the various stages of manufacture. *Operation instructions* to each machine specify the timetable of jobs to be undertaken.

Finally when the work is commenced, there must be some means of reporting back to the manager on progress and any difficulties which may be encountered. In the light of developments, the manager must modify his plans.

Computer Scheme

Dates can be represented in the computer by the week number; the weeks of the year being numbered from 1 to 52. Some firms may find it more convenient to number the days of the year from 1 to 365.

As stated in the previous section, the management must start the planning for the year by specifying a timetable for the completion of finished products. This is punched into cards, each week having a week number and a product list indicating numbers required of each. The cards are then used as input in a computer operation to produce a second timetable stating parts needed and date when required. This timetable is printed out and is also recorded on magnetic tape for the next stage. This next stage is the printing of machine loading statements for manufactured parts and dated orders for bought parts. Again the information is recorded on tape. Upon examining the machine loading statement, the manager may wish to make amendments and those are punched into cards so that the computer information can be corrected. This ends the production planning and nothing further is required of the computer until the year is about to commence. The computer then produces the works documentation for, say, the first three weeks. Route sheets are printed but material requisitions and operation instructions are punched into cards by the computer. A special machine is available which can read a card and print the corresponding characters on the top of the card. This machine is used to make the card output intelligible to the factory workers. The reason for using cards instead of printed paper will be made clear shortly.

Once the year is under way, the computer is used to monitor progress. The work documentation goes out to the factory. Route sheets go to the machines where production is to start. Material requisition cards go to the stores and accompany the materials to the machines. On arrival at the machines, the cards are returned to the computer room. Operation instructions cards go to the machines and when an operation is complete, the card is returned to the computer room while the partly manufactured material passes to the next machine with the route sheet. At the daily computer session, all returned cards are fed into the computer and they enable the computer to compare actual progress with intended progress. Management reports can then be issued indicating points at which production is falling behind schedule. In the light of these failures, the work schedule is amended. Works documentation is produced weekly in the light of the latest situation. The rapidity with which the computer can produce output is very useful in this application.

The technique of using cards to inform the computer of progress can also be used in connection with outside orders. When the computer prints an order to be sent to a supplier, it also punches a card. The card is sent to the stores. When the supplies are received, the card is returned to the computer. In this way, the computer can keep a check on deliveries and can mention any overdue orders in the management report.

The computer procedures in production control are not essentially different from those we have considered in previous chapters. The only procedure of any interest is that used in the initial stage of breaking down products into their component parts. For this a bill of material file is prepared beforehand. Each record in this file is the bill of material for one of the company's products and there is a record for every finished product. Each record indicates the assemblies, sub-assemblies and parts needed for the product, together with the number of weeks before completion when they are required. Each assembly, sub-assembly and part has a catalogue number and it also has a 'level of complexity' number. This latter is 1 for parts, 2 for sub-assemblies and 3 for assemblies. Both these numbers are mentioned in the bill of material file.

For the first computer run, the bill of material file is set on a tape unit and another tape is set to received information. Since the bill of material file is not altered in this run, it is removed unchanged at the end. The proposed production program, indicating the timetable of requirements for finished products, is punched into cards which are placed in the computer's card reader after being sorted into correct product order. The program causes the cards to be read and for each required product, the bill of material is located in the file. Information concerning the needed components is transferred to the other magnetic tape until every required product has been dealt with. The information on this tape consists of records, each one of which refers to an assembly, sub-assembly or part. Each record has four segments giving catalogue number of component, its level of complexity number, number required and date required.

In the second computer run, the resulting magnetic tape is sorted so that the components are in catalogue order.

For the third computer run, a file is used containing bills of material for assemblies. The tape coming forward from the second run is set on a tape unit as also is another tape to receive information. The program causes the tape from the second run to be read. Each record referring to sub-assemblies or parts is passed un-changed to the receiving tape. For an assembly, distin-guished by its level of complexity number 3, the bill of material is located in the file. In this way assemblies are broken down exactly as were products in the first run. The needed sub-assemblies and parts are recorded on the receiving tape.

The fourth run sorts this tape into catalogue order. The fifth run is like the third but a bill of material file for sub-assemblies is used. At the end of this run all information refers only to parts. Finally a sixth run is used to sort the information into date order to form the timetable of parts required. This timetable, on magnetic tape, passes forward to computer runs for machine loading and so on.

The above procedure may appear cumbersome, but it must be remembered that this initial stage of the pro-duction programme is only processed once every two or three months at most. The consumption of computer time is thus negligible.

D

Quotations

So far in this chapter, we have been considering a type of
production which involves the assembly of parts into
standard finished products, i.e., the company makes a
substantial number of each product. The price which will
be charged for the product can be decided by the management and reviewed every few months in the light
of increasing costs.

There is another type of production where the finished
product incorporates a number of variations on a basic
theme according to the requirements of the customer. It
follows that this production is only undertaken after a
firm order has been received. Also, in general, the order
will not be confirmed until a satisfactory price has been
agreed. The procedure is that upon receiving the initial
enquiry from the customer, the company works out the
price it would ask if the work were undertaken. This price,
called the *quotation*, is sent to the customer for his consideration. If he is satisfied, he confirms the order and the
work is put in hand. It will be apparent that not all initial
orders will be confirmed and so some of the clerical work
involved in preparing quotations is wasted. This is an
inevitable feature of this type of business.

The first application of a computer to this type of work
was made in the United States in the early sixties. General
Electric used a computer in connection with its manufacture of heavy switch gear, transformers and power plants.
Westinghouse followed with an application to its orders
for heavy duty motors and generators. In Germany the
firm of Voith applied a computer to its manufacture of
paper machines, turbines, torque converters and gear
boxes. The advantage of computer processing of orders
is that clerical delays are avoided and the customer
receives a quotation in a very short space of time.

In order to explain the application in more detail we shall consider a simple and fictitious example. A company undertakes the manufacture of metal storage tanks for liquids. The tanks are cylindrical in shape. Three diameters are available and the length of the cylinder can be specified by the customer. A typical tank is shown in Fig. 4.1. Connecting pieces C can be fixed anywhere on the tank so that pipes P can lead into it. Two diameters of pipe can be catered for, but pipes are not provided by

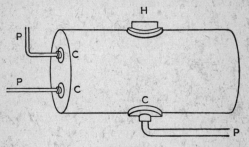

Fig. 4.1

the company. An inspection hatch H can be placed anywhere along the top of the tank.

The tanks are constructed from cylindrical metal tubes, of the three available diameters, which are cut to the required length of the tank. Two circles are cut from flat metal plate to form the ends of the tank which are then welded to the tube. Fitting the hatch and connecting pieces involves cutting holes in the tank and welding on the parts. From suppliers are obtained the three types of tube, the flat metal plate, the hatches and connecting pieces. Three types of hatch are needed to fit the three types of tube. Eight types of connecting piece are needed: four for each pipe diameter; the four being for connection to flat plate or to the three diameters of tube.

The cost of a tank is worked out as follows. First there is the cost of materials. There are three different costs for the three tube diameters and the cost of the tube is proportional to its length. There are three different costs for the flat ends depending on the diameter. Hatches are all the same price and there are two prices for connecting pieces depending on the pipe diameter. Next come cutting costs. In the construction of the tank, there will be three of these depending on tube diameter. There will be a cost for the hatch hole and two costs for the connecting pieces depending on pipe diameter. Finally there are welding costs: three for tube diameter, one for hatch and two for connecting pieces.

Each of the different costs involved in making the tank can be recorded on magnetic tape to form a file of costs. This file can be kept up to date as costs change. When a customer sends in an order, the following information is punched into cards:

(1) diameter of tank
(2) length of tank
(3) number of hatches
(4) number of connecting pieces for small pipes
(5) number of connecting pieces for large pipes

A program causes this information to be read into the computer, after which it is a simple matter for it to calculate the total cost by reference to the file of costs. The total cost is printed out. The sale price, stated in the quotation to the customer, is this total cost together with an extra amount to cover administrative and 'overhead' expenses and a profit margin. The sale price requires a human decision because there are a number of factors to take into account. These include the extent of previous orders from the customer and the amount of competition from other firms.

In some applications of this type, the computer can go on to prepare works documentation once the order is confirmed. More often, however, the drawing office prepares the detailed working instructions as geometrical considerations are involved, as in the example of our storage tank.

Distribution

The main application of computers in the distribution area of a company's activities is to the clerical work associated with the operation of a fleet of vehicles used to deliver the company's products. Not all companies have such fleets. Many prefer to use government operated postal or other transport services. Then again, there are companies which specialize entirely in the operating of road transport vehicles.

The operation of a transport fleet gives rise to the clerical activities associated with any business such as payroll and accounting. An important aspect of the accounting is the recording of fuel, maintenance and replacement costs.

A new clerical activity which arises in operating the fleet is the planning of the journeys and loads for the individual vehicles. On the basis of orders received from customers, for each working day the planner is presented with a number of points on the map (i.e., the customers' premises) and a load associated with each point; the distribution of points will be different each day. His task is to join together the points to form one or more 'strings'. The length of a string is limited by the load which one vehicle can carry and there may also be a time limit if the deliveries are to be completed in one day. For each string, a vehicle starts from the depot and proceeds directly to the customer at one end of the string. It then makes deliveries to the customers in the string and finally returns to the depot.

For a computer to undertake this clerical activity, a method is required by which it can form the strings of customers. The technique will be considered in Chapter 10. Once a program fragment for this is available, the preparation of lists of customers for each journey can be performed by the computer at the same time as the invoice procedure considered in Chapter 3. Also, by marking each invoice with a journey reference number, the invoice can be used in the warehouse not only to make up the customer's order but also to channel the goods to be loaded into the appropriate vehicle.

Product Support

An interesting application of computers to product support occurs in connection with aero-engines. Engines must be periodically removed from service so that overhauls can be effected. In addition to this, service problems occasionally arise due to damage from an external source or a fault in the engine itself, and these involve additional unscheduled maintenance. In order to accumulate as much knowledge as possible on engine behaviour, Rolls-Royce maintains computer records of all its engines operating in civil and military aircraft all over the world. Altogether about 14,000 engines are involved. The record of an engine includes its hours of operation, history of modification, replacements and breakdowns as well as details of aircraft type and conditions in which it operates. From this vast store of information, continually up-dated with details coming in, the computer can extract statistics on the reliability of different engine types. Weak parts of engines can be located so that research can be directed towards improvements in design. In this way, steadily higher levels of safety and efficiency can be achieved and Rolls-Royce is able to maintain its world lead in civil aircraft engines.

5 Banking and Giro

That part of our capital known as the *City of London* is made up of headquarters offices of large companies and of the exchanges in commodities. In addition, there are companies and institutions concerned specifically with financial matters. Taken together, they form one of the world's most important commercial centres and they contribute, in no small measure, to the economic prosperity of the country as a whole.

In order that the services offered by this centre shall continue to be of the highest standard, computer methods are being introduced, where they are appropriate. In view of the national importance of the specialized financial organizations and their bearing upon all business activities, we shall devote this and the following two chapters to their study. We shall find that the computer techniques developed in previous chapters will stand us in good stead and it will be necessary only to describe the various financial activities so that the role of the computer can be appreciated.

History of Finance

The money which we use consists of coins and pound notes. We regard these two forms of money as equivalent and we change one for the other without thought or question. Their origins in history are, however, entirely separate.

Coins made their appearance in the eighth century B.C.

as the end product in the development of barter trade. Primitive barter consists of exchanging goods for goods and in the absence of money, this was the only type of trade that was possible. Dealings were much facilitated, however, by considering the value of goods in relation to some standard item. There are indications that such things as basins and axes were used as such standard items in some places. Once the technique of weighing things had been mastered, weight became a significant factor affecting value. In this way metals, rather than finished products, became standards of value and in this respect gold, silver and copper have held pride of place throughout history. Deals were effected by exchanging goods for a weighed amount of metal. The final development was the use of lumps of metal marked with an impression indicating that they were of a particular weight. This obviated the need to weigh out metal at each transaction. Thus a *coin* may be defined as a piece of precious metal stamped with some mark or type or inscription showing that it is issued by some authority which guarantees its weight and purity. The early technique for small coins was to place a weighed amount of molten metal on a flat surface and to press a stamp on to it. This produced a flat rounded form which set the fashion for subsequent coins made by moulding. Coins have exerted a fascination on men's minds beyond their original purpose as a medium of exchange, and they have been collected and hoarded throughout history, as they also are today.

Coins came into general use only gradually, and in Rome fines were extracted in cattle down to the end of the fifth century B.C. With the introduction of coins, the money lending and money changing trades came into being. But loans of goods were recorded much earlier. In Babylon, loans were made by the temples in 2000 B.C.

In 575 B.C. a private firm, the Igibi bank, was making loans and receiving deposits with interest. By the fourth century B.C. in Greece, financial activities had reached a high degree of development and temples, public bodies and private firms were involved. Following the collapse of the Roman Empire, the financial traditions of the ancient world fell into disuse. The laws against usury also limited financial activities.

When deposit banking re-emerged in medieval Europe, the transfer of bank credit was through oral instruction in the presence of witnesses. The legal doctrine of negotiability evolved only gradually from the sixteenth to the eighteenth centuries. To further trade in the medieval world, fairs were held from time to time, just as they are today. The most famous place for these fairs was Champagne, and special financial arrangements were made for the promotion of the dealings which the fairs gave rise to. The system, though ingenious and highly important in its day, involved neither deposits nor credit creation, so it did not contribute much to the evolution of modern banking.

Being away from these activities, developments in England were much slower. The direct ancestors of modern banks were the goldsmiths who acted as money-lenders by lending their own money. Goldsmiths also accepted deposits for safe keeping, since they usually had, in any case, to provide themselves with a strong room to protect the materials of their trade from thieves. In accepting a valuable object or gold coins for safe keeping, the goldsmith would issue a receipt on a piece of paper. The depositor, in his subsequent dealings often found it more convenient and safer to 'pay' for goods by merely handing over the goldsmith's receipt to the seller. Early in the seventeenth century, these deposit receipts were circulating in place of coins and so became the first

English bank notes. Soon the goldsmiths began to issue notes not against the deposit of coin but also by way of loan and this was the beginning of fractional-reserve banking in England.

The Bank of England was formed in 1694 as a private firm, mainly for the purpose of financing the activities of the Government. The bank worked closely with the Government from the start and soon became a national institution. It was formally nationalized in 1946.

There were few private banks outside London until after 1750, but the industrial revolution gave rise to the need for a developed financial system and banks sprang up all over the country. The wars with France of 1793–1815 imposed a great strain on the English monetary system and in 1825 occurred one of the most violent financial crises of the century. During this period, the need for proper control of banking and financial activities was realized, but this did not prevent economic crises from occurring with increasing severity until well into the present century, causing much human misery. It would be rash to say that we now understand these matters sufficiently well to be able to avoid their recurrence. The end of the nineteenth century saw the amalgamation of the small banks and by 1918 there remained only a few banks, each having a nationwide network of branches. This arrangement has worked well for fifty years, but the arrival of computers is now creating the need for further organizational changes in British banking.

The printed cheque appeared in 1730, but it was another century before it began to assume its present importance in financial transactions.

Turning to insurance, marine insurance was practised by the Italian traders of the fifteenth century. Life assurance in England existed in 1583. Fire insurance originated in its modern form following the great fire of London in 1666. Other types of insurance have developed since 1850.

Money and Inflation

From the history of the development of money, we see that, originally, the value of a coin was the value of the metal of which it was composed. The paper bank notes had no value in themselves, but they were promises by the bank to pay the stated amount in coin. This promise is still printed on pound notes, though it is now largely devoid of meaning owing to the changed nature of money in modern times.

Once mankind had conceived the notion of value as represented by metal it was a short step further to considering value as an abstraction, separate from any particular material medium. Once this idea had been accepted, money could be issued consisting of coins and notes, both being only symbolic of value. Provided the issuing authority had sufficient power to impose this money and provided the public would accept it with confidence, then it could be used satisfactorily as a medium of exchange. Everybody alive today has been brought up on this concept of money.

Now that money has been detached from its original metallic basis, its equivalent in terms of goods is somewhat arbitrary and is in fact determined by the issuing authority. Further, the equivalent of money in terms of goods can alter with the passage of time, again under the influence of the issuing authority. There are three possibilities: money can buy more or it can buy less or it can buy the same amount of goods as time passes. It has come to be established that money buys less as time goes on. This process is called *inflation*. The issuing authority does this by printing more and more notes and passing them into general circulation, e.g., as payment for government purchases. The more bank notes people have, the more ready they are to spend them and this enables retailers to put up their prices. This is the mechanism by which inflation occurs. Paper money is pumped into circulation, much as air is pumped into a tyre to inflate it!

In England, money is issued only by the Bank of England. As a result of inflation, the pound loses true value at a rate of about 7 per cent each year. This inflation process meets with general approval and we must mention its principal advantages.

First of all it must be noted that money is intended as a medium of exchange and as such it is largely used. Thus, the employee spends most of his wages on current needs, so long-term inflation has no effect on this spending. The first advantage has already been mentioned, namely, the Government can pay for some of its requirements with new notes and so, in effect, gets them for nothing. Further, the Government can borrow money now and pay it back later when it has lost value. Large companies can do the same. Another advantage is that trade unions can more readily claim pay increases for their members and employers can more readily concede to them. In return for these advantages, there has to be a loser; he is the man who wishes to save his money for future use. We shall turn our attention to him in Chapter 7.

It will be noticed that the price of a largely permanent object, such as a house, tends to go up and up. This is because the cost of construction of such objects increases, like everything else, due to inflation.

Symbolic money, subject to a slow and controlled inflation, is the end product of the long history of money. It serves its purpose very well within particular countries and the problems which money still presents are concerned with dealings between one country and another.

Current Account Banking

We have seen that English banking started with the *deposit* of money for safe keeping and this is still one of its main purposes. Money deposited at the bank by a customer goes into the bank's safe and the amount is recorded in the customer's account. The accounts used for this purpose are called *current accounts*, the idea being that customers use these accounts for popping money in and out to suit their convenience. Savings accounts and savings banks will be mentioned in the following chapter.

Once a customer has established an account at a bank, he subsequently indicates his wishes by means of *cheques*. These are essentially written messages to the bank indicating to whom money in the account is to be transferred. Books of cheques for use by the customer are provided by the bank. Thus, to get money out of the bank himself, a customer writes a cheque indicating the amount he desires and on presenting it at the bank, the required sum of money is paid over. To pay money to another person, the customer writes a cheque indicating the person's name and the amount of money; he then gives the cheque to the person, who can take it to the bank to be cashed. Arrangements exist for the interchange of cheques between different banks. The person may not wish to draw the money, but instead he may wish to have it credited to his own bank account.

If the customer has to make payments on a regular basis, he can give *standing orders* to the bank and it will arrange the necessary transfer of money from the customer's account without the need for him to write cheques every time.

Small charges are made for these current account facilities.

Loans

The basis of all loans is that after an agreed period of time, the amount of the loan will be repaid to the lender, together with *interest*. Interest is an extra amount which the borrower pays to the lender for the favour of the loan. The deal is not without risk to the lender, who may require some assurance that the loan can be repaid. Interest is usually measured as a percentage of the amount of the loan per year. Thus, suppose *A* lends *B* the sum of £100 at 10 per cent per year for a period of six months. Then at the end of the six months, *B* must repay *A* the sum of £105.

Banks will lend money to their customers for private or business purposes.

The increasing use of cheques for settling financial matters has given rise to a situation, which did not exist in ancient times, in which banks effectively create money. This is called *bank credit*. The explanation is as follows. Suppose we have a bank and two of its customers, *A* and *B*. Customer *A* goes to the bank and asks for a loan of £500. The bank agrees to make the loan and so writes £500 into *A*'s account. Next *A* goes to *B* and arranges to buy his car for £500. As payment, *A* writes a cheque in favour of *B* which *B* deposits at the bank. As a result, the bank deducts the £500 from *A*'s account and writes it into *B*'s account. Of course, *A* is still in debt to the bank and must pay interest on the loan until he repays it. The point to note, however, is that the sale of a car has taken place without the need for any money to change hands. The sale has been effected merely by the juggling of bank accounts. The bank has not really lent any money at all, but is nonetheless collecting interest from *A*. Also, since the bank's action has resulted in a sale, it has had the same effect on the economy as if it had provided *A* with cash. Is there any limit on the extent to which banks can create credit in this way? The answer is that there is definitely a limit because there is the risk that B may wish to draw out his money. The bank must therefore have enough cash on hand to be able to pay any customer who wishes to make a withdrawal. On the other hand, most customers are happy to leave some money in the bank, so the bank can safely lend credit in excess of the money it has received in deposits. This is *fractional-reserve* banking.

Bank credit in recent years has been restricted by the Government as part of its policy of controlling the extent of economic development in the country.

Computerized Banking

Since banks are concerned with keeping accounts, the computer techniques are essentially those described in Chapter 3. A complication does arise where interest has to be calculated, but we shall leave consideration of this until the next chapter.

In the computer scheme which has been introduced at Westminster Bank, the computers are located at the headquarters in London. Customers still have their local branches of the bank through which they deal. Details of their accounts, however, are in the computers in London. Details of deposits and withdrawals made by customers are punched into paper tape at the branches. The branches are grouped into local areas, each of which has a Datel link to headquarters. After the day's business at the branches, the tapes are taken to the Datel terminal, usually located at the main branch in the area, and the information is transmitted to London so that the computers can update the accounts. The computers print out statements of the customers' accounts when required and these are returned to the branches.

Plans are in hand to link branches directly to the computers using Datel links.

The branch organization of the bank must remain so that customers can have access to their bank managers for help and advice on financial matters. Also, the issuing of loans will usually be decided at branch level as so many human factors enter into the decision that it hardly admits of computerization.

Using appropriate paper, the computers can print out cheques when required. Such an application occurs in connection with the Westminster Bank Payroll Service when the employee chooses to be paid by cheque.

Where a customer places standing orders, these are stored in a computer file so that the customer's wishes can be effected from time to time.

Perhaps the most interesting feature of computer banking is the method by which cheques are handled. To explain this, we must first look at the method used prior to the advent of the computer. Suppose that A is a customer at bank X and that B is a customer at bank Y. Now let us see what happens when A gives or sends B a cheque for £100 and B pays the cheque in at his branch of bank Y. The cheque must cause three things to happen: A's account must be reduced by £100; B's account must be increased by £100; and arrangements must be made for £100, in cash or credit, to pass from bank X to bank Y. These matters are most efficiently dealt with by each bank having a *central clearing department* in London. The procedure regarding B's cheque is then as follows. At B's branch of bank Y, B's account is adjusted. The cheque is then sent by post, together with others which have been paid in during the day, to the central clearing department of bank Y. The branch will have sorted cheques according to the bank of issue. At the central clearing department, the cheques are separated and sent to the central clearing departments of the appropriate banks where they are sorted according to the branch of issue. The sorted cheques are then returned to the branches. Thus, *B*'s cheque finds its way back to *A*'s branch of bank *X*. Here it is used to adjust *A*'s account, then the cancelled cheque is returned to *A*, thus assuring him that his wishes have been carried out.

The advent of the computer has enabled cheque sorting at the clearing departments to be put on an automatic basis. This requires that the information on the cheque be put in a form which can be read by machinery. This is done by *encoding* the cheque with special characters along the bottom edge. These characters, mainly numbers, are rather strange but are readable. The information which a cheque conveys consists of five parts:

   (1) serial number
   (2) bank and branch number
   (3) account number
   (4) amount
   (5) name of payee

The serial number identifies the particular cheque. The bank and branch number identifies the branch of issue from all other branches of all banks. The account number identifies the customer.

It will be seen that parts (1) to (3) do not depend on the amount of the cheque nor to whom it is paid. Consequently, they can be encoded on to the cheque before it is given to the customer. The customer, *A*, writes the amount and name of payee, *B*, on the cheque in the usual way. He sends it to *B* who pays it into his branch of bank *Y*. Here it is used to adjust *B*'s account and it is encoded with the amount of the cheque. Each branch of each bank has an encoding machine for this purpose and since

February 1968 all banks have agreed to encode amounts on each other's cheques. Although cheques issued by the banks are of differing shapes and sizes, it is agreed that the amount is encoded in the bottom right corner in all cases. Thus each cheque, which is paid in at the branch of a bank, is placed in an encoding machine and the amount written on the cheque is also encoded on to it by pressing keys on the machine. The name of the payee is not encoded as it is of no interest after B's account has been adjusted.

The cheques are sent to London, as before, and our cheque reaches the central clearing department of bank X. Here it is put with other cheques through a sorting machine attached to a small computer. The machine reads the encoded characters and conveys the information to the computer, where it is stored on magnetic tape. The machine also sorts the cheques into branches for subsequent dispatch. This sorting is not done in one operation as there may be 1500 branches of bank X and half a million cheques to be sorted each day! The magnetic tape is later transferred on to a larger computer where the information is used to update the customers' accounts.

This cheque handling procedure is complicated by elaborate checking at each stage and also by arrangements for torn and damaged cheques.

It will be seen that the technique of encoding cheques is equivalent to punching the information into cards but the need for the card is obviated. The encoded characters are printed on the cheques with an ink containing a magnetic material. The sorting machine reads the encoded characters by a magnetic method, but optical reading techniques can also be used with these characters. In the future, we may well see this encoding technique replacing the traditional punched card input for computer information.

In recent years, banks have introduced credit card schemes. The associated accounting has, in most cases, been computerized from the start. The accounting for travellers' cheques is also being undertaken on computers.

Linking the banks together in the computer age is the Inter-Bank Computer Bureau. This is a small organization situated in London, and its purpose is to deal with the accounting arising from transactions between banks. Equipped with a computer installation, the Bureau can deal with information provided by the banks on magnetic tape, so the need for documents is completely eliminated.

National Giro

At the time of writing the *National Giro* has recently gone into operation. It is computerized from the start. It is a Government institution and it will compete with the commercial banks, although only in the field of current-account banking.

The aim is to provide a method of transferring money which is a good deal cheaper than any other postal method. Suppose *A* wishes to pay *B* the sum of £100. If *A* lives near to *B* he can pay in cash and this costs nothing. If, however, *A* lives far away from *B*, then there is at least the postage involved when *A* informs *B*, no matter what method of transferring the money is used. By using Giro, even this postage is largely saved; the transfer of the money is effected without charge.

To use the Giro most cheaply, *A* and *B* must both have Giro accounts. Any person over 16 can open an account with a deposit of £5. Account holders are provided with transfer forms and envelopes for which a small charge is made. To effect the transfer, *A* fills in a transfer form and sends it in an envelope to the Giro Centre. On the day the envelope reaches the Centre, the transfer is effected and the form is sent by post to *B*. If *A* wishes, he can write a message to *B* on the back of the transfer form.

In principle, everyone can have a Giro account and so all payments could be made by Giro transfer and no cash need ever be used. However, owing to the slight charges, it is still more convenient to use cash for everyday personal expenses.

It is hoped that the Giro will pay for itself as the large amount of money deposited in it can be invested at a high rate of interest. Giro pays no interest on deposits and overdrafts are not allowed. Account holders are provided with statements at frequent intervals.

The efficient Giro system just described is supplemented by other facilities but the charges are more substantial. For this purpose, Post Offices act as 'branches'. It is possible to pay in cash and cheques and to make cash withdrawals. It is possible for firms sending out bills to attach Giro forms for the convenience of their customers. Standing orders are carried out without charge. Directories of Giro account holders are published at regular intervals. Eventually, links will be established with Giro systems in other countries.

The Giro Centre is located in Liverpool. This position was chosen as it has efficient rail and postal connections with all parts of the country. The envelopes provided to account holders have different colours to identify the locality. This enables the Centre to process envelopes from distant parts early in the day, thus ensuring the efficiency of the service to all parts of the country. The envelopes are opened at the Centre then the forms are checked and encoded. The forms are then microfilmed for record purposes, after which the information is read into a computer for the adjustment of the accounts and the printing of statements. These statements are microfilmed before being associated with the transfer forms and dispatched by post.

It is hoped that the National Giro will make a significant contribution to financial efficiency in the age of computers.

6 Insurance and Building Societies

Human beings and their activities are inevitably subject to dangers. When these dangers result in catastrophe, the financial consequences, at least, can be greatly alleviated by insurance. Thus it is that the wise person, whether in his private activities or in his business, guards against such misfortunes by taking out insurance policies with reliable insurance companies. Sound insurance forms the basis for large-scale business activity which could not otherwise be undertaken.

Nature of Contract

An *insurance policy* is a legal contract between the *insurer* and the *insured*. The insurer is usually an insurance company, being a company which specializes in providing insurance as will now be explained. The insured is the person or company which requires financial *protection* from the consequences of the dangers to which his or its activities are subject. The contract always specifies an amount of time over which the contract is effective, e.g., during the year 1971 or during next Easter holiday. The contract also specifies the catastrophes or mishaps which are *covered*. The contract goes on to state that if any of the said catastrophes or mishaps occurs in the said period of time, then the insurer will pay the insured a fixed amount of money called the *benefit*. Prior to issue of this contract, the insured pays the insurer a fee called the *premium*.

In the business area, a wide variety of situations require

protection and policies are available. A standard policy is available for farmers, for example, against the damage to crops caused by hailstones. Where a standard policy is not available, an insurance company will usually offer a special contract to cover the situation.

In the area of the private individual, available policies divide into those which cover the person's life or health and those which cover his property and his liability to others.

Personal liability can arise in cases where a person, of himself, accidentally causes injury to others. Such events are rare and a policy is available for a premium of about £0·50 per year. An example is the case of a person who causes an accident by dangerously walking in the road.

Liability is far more likely to occur from a person's property or its use. Thus, a car owner needs a policy to guard against the dangers which threaten the car itself and also one to guard against the dangers to the persons travelling in his car and to other persons or vehicles using the road.

Household insurance is perhaps the most important type of policy involving property. This is because of the high cost of accommodation which is a feature of countries having a high level of economic development. The wise person must thus insure in order to protect his not inconsiderable investment in his home. There is a choice of policies for the householder. The cheapest offers protection only against fire. For a slightly higher premium, cover can be obtained against the ravages of storm and tempest and also against trivialities such as the collapse of television aerials and the breakage of glass. Until recently, cover was not available against flood damage but has now been made available as a result of public clamour. The premium for a year's protection depends on the value of the house; the rate is about

£0·10 for each £100 of value. Thus a house valued at
£2000 would require a premium of £2 per year. The
contents of a house can be insured separately against fire
and burglary.

Household insurance illustrates well the limitations of
insurance. There are some eventualities which an insurance company will not cover. Thus, many aspects of
the householder's cover do not apply if the house is left
empty for any length of time. It is not possible to insure
against things which are of a slow and continuous nature
like decay and subsidence, nor against faulty construction
and workmanship. Further, an insurance company will
not replace old by new, so the cost of repairing damage to
an old house would only be partly paid for by the company. It is important for the insured to understand fully
the limitations which apply to his own policy. In general,
an insurance company offers protection against dangers
which are small compared with the whole community. It
cannot offer protection against the effects of war or of
armed insurrection, whether war be declared or not.

Turning to risks to life and health, insurance policies
are available offering a specified sum of money in the
event of death or of accident resulting in particular
injuries. Another type of policy offers a weekly payment
in the event of loss of earnings caused by sickness or accident. It is important at this point to note that an insurance
contract lasts only for the period of time stated and there
is no obligation upon insurer or insured to renew the
contract at the end. There is an exception to this in the
case of a permanent sickness and accident policy. Under
such a policy, the insurer, but not the insured, is obliged
to renew the policy each year until the insured reaches
retiring age. Thus, if the insured becomes entirely in-
capacitated from working, the company must continue
the weekly payments for the rest of his working life.

Strangely, such policies have little appeal and few companies offer them.

The policies so far considered usually run for a year and in general will be *renewed* for a further year provided both parties are agreeable. Policies which are for a more limited duration and which are not normally renewed relate to travel and holidays. A person travelling abroad may wish to insure against medical expenses whereas at home he would regard the free National Health Service as offering adequate cover. Such policies limit the behaviour of the insured while on the trip but for higher premiums certain dangerous sporting activities can be covered. Travel insurance can also be obtained against loss of personal effects and against losses if the trip has to be cancelled.

For all the insurance policies we have considered so far, and we have but touched on a few of those available, the activities of the insurance company consist of collecting premiums, issuing policies (i.e., contracts) and investigating and paying *claims* in the event of insured persons suffering loss in the circumstances specified. Outgoing payments are thus claims and the running costs of the company. Income consists of the premiums, and as with any company, the profit is the excess of income over expenditure. If total claims were unduly large, the company might be unable to pay and the collapse of the company would follow. The same result could occur if the company offered policies at unduly low premiums. In the financial world there are few things more unnerving than the collapse of an insurance company. Recently, legislation has been passed to ensure an even stricter Government watch on insurance activities.

Life Assurance

A very popular type of policy offered by insurance
companies is called *life assurance* and it is a combination
of insurance against death with straightforward regular
saving. This idea is illustrated by the following example.
The insured person agrees to make a monthly payment of
£1 for a period of ten years. The company saves the
money for him but also offers, in the event of the death
of the insured, to make the total saving, £120, available
upon death. In addition, the company offers either a fixed
rate of interest on the savings or, alternatively, an
unspecified 'profit'. If the insured outlives the ten years,
then he is alive to collect his savings together with the
accumulated interest or profit. The insurance company is
able to offer this type of policy because the cost of insur-
ing the total savings against death is small. The company
actually invests the money at a high rate of interest; the
difference between this interest rate and that offered to the
insured effectively pays for the insurance and also yields a
profit to the company. From the insured person's point of
view, he gets financial cover against his death as soon as
he has signed the policy. He also has the assurance that
if he lives, he will collect his savings with interest. If
circumstances change, he is free to discontinue the policy
at any time and withdraw most of the money.

Before a life assurance policy is issued, the person must
undergo a medical examination to see that he is not in
immediate danger of dying. A medical examination is also
necessary for permanent sickness insurance but not for
sickness and accident insurance covering one year.

In the case of life assurance, in addition to the activities
of the company described above for insurance, there is
the job of maintaining accounts for the insured persons
and of investing the resulting money.

Computer Applications

The Sun Alliance & London Insurance Group is in the gradual process of transferring its clerical activities on to computers. In addition to its headquarters building south of London, this company has about seventy local offices throughout the country.

Under present arrangements, insurance policies are issued at the local offices and premiums are collected there. The payment of most claims is also arranged at the local offices. However, details of all policies issued are sent to the computer department at headquarters where they are punched into cards then recorded on magnetic tape by the computer. This involves the storage on tape of four and a half million records which requires quite a 'library' of tape reels. Amendments to policies are sent to the computer department as also are policy cancellations. These details are used to update the records. A printout is obtained of all changes to the records and this is sent back to the local office as a check. Apart from maintaining a magnetic record of all policies, the computer also issues annual printouts for each policy about a month before renewal is due. These printouts consist of a printer page divided by a perforated line down the middle. One side is a renewal reminder and the other side is a renewal receipt. The printouts are sent to the appropriate local offices where the renewal reminder is torn off and sent in a window envelope to the insured. If the insured decides to renew, he sends in the money whereupon the receipt side of the printout is sent back to him. A renewal payment does not involve any communication from the local office to the computer because, since the policy is continuing unchanged, no modification of the magnetic record is necessary. The mere printing out of recorded information may seem a trivial task for a computer but it must also be remembered that in some months there are half a million printouts. It would be quite a task if they had to be prepared by clerks. This emphasizes an important benefit of the computer: it can relieve the human being of clerical chores of an annual nature which are devoid of interest but nonetheless have to be done.

Future plans will involve the transfer of the accounting from the local offices to headquarters. Insured persons will then make their payments to headquarters either directly or via the local offices. The accounts will be handled by the computer. The need for the local offices will still remain to provide personal advice to customers and for the investigation of claims.

The life assurance side of the business is already handled at headquarters by the computer. This involves magnetic recording of the savings accounts of customers just as in the case of building societies as will be explained later in this chapter.

Another application of computers in insurance is the preparation of up-to-date statistics relating to claims. For example, how frequently are houses damaged by fire and what is the average cost of the damage? This is no academic question; the answer to it determines the level of premiums which must be charged for fire insurance. Now the risk of fire in houses is very small and when a fire does occur, the local brigade can usually get it rapidly under control. These facts have enabled premiums to be kept at a very low level. In other areas of insurance, however, the picture is entirely different. What is the effect on the accident rate of the increasing congestion on the roads? Or again, are modern industrial processes leading to an improvement in safety standards, or not? The answers to questions like these can be obtained by feeding details of claims into the computer. For each year, the computer can easily calculate the number of claims per

100 policies for each type of insurance. Comparison of the figures from one year to the next indicates any changing trend. More detailed statistics such as accident rates in town and country districts can also be worked out. Similar calculations for life assurance policies give the trend in the life expectancy of the population.

Building Societies

Customers at banks, in addition to their current accounts, can usually open savings accounts upon which interest is paid. Some banks specialize entirely in this type of account and are then called *savings banks*. Their concern is not with transferring money but with investing it.

Some savings banks specialize in investments of a risky nature and offer a high rate of interest. These banks, also referred to as *finance houses*, invest their customers' money in such things as hire purchase and export financing. Other savings banks specialize in safe investment and offer a more modest rate of interest. All these banks are introducing computers for their accounting.

Of the banks specializing in safe investment, the *building societies* deserve particular mention, owing to the large amount of wealth which is involved in housing in all industrialized countries. This wealth is provided in large measure through building societies although insurance companies and banks also invest their money in this way.

The need for investment arises from the fact that owing to the high prices of houses, many potential purchasers are unable to afford them. The difficulty is overcome by a building society agreeing to provide most of the money on the basis of a *mortgage*. This is a legal contract, a loan agreement, but it gives the society the right to sell the house in the event of the purchaser failing to make the agreed repayments. The repayments consist of the money lent together with interest and are spread over 25 years or so. Out of the repayments from mortgages, the society can pay interest to its customers on their deposits. Interest is frequently paid by means of *dividend warrants*, which are essentially the same as cheques, and these warrants can be printed by computer.

Computer accounting of savings accounts differs from current accounting in that interest has to be calculated each time there is a deposit or withdrawal. If the days of the financial year are numbered 1 to 365, then let the savings account of customer A remain unaltered at p pounds, from day x to day y. What interest has accumulated in this period if the interest rate is i per cent per year? The interest on p pounds for a year would be

$$pi/100$$

but we are considering not a year but $y - x$ days, which is a fraction

$$(y - x)/365$$

of a year. The interest is this fraction of the annual interest and is thus given by

$$pi(y - x)/36500.$$

This must be calculated and added to the p pounds in the account before any other adjustment is made on day y.

7 The Stock Exchange

Notwithstanding the importance of the financial organizations which we have considered in the previous two chapters, the Stock Exchange must be regarded as the real heart of the City. The view of the activities from the Visitors' Gallery is a sight which has to be seen to be believed. It is a human ants' nest. The movements of some two thousand men around the floor seem utterly confused but, as we shall see, they result in a highly efficient market in the shares of companies and business enterprises spread throughout the world. Without such a market, modern industrial activity, as we know it, would not be possible.

The activity seen on the floor of the Stock Exchange is backed up by work in the offices of numerous specialist firms and the dealings on the Exchange give rise to prodigious amounts of recording and calculation, much of which is now being undertaken by computers.

Company Shares

Before considering the activities of the Stock Exchange in more detail, it will be necessary for us to examine the ways in which companies are financed.

Many businesses start as small retail enterprises, owned and run by one man possibly with the aid of some labour. By hard work, thrift and a fair measure of luck, such a man can slowly build up his business without the need of anybody else's money. There are other circumstances,

however, in which a company sees the opportunity to
expand, based on definite orders for its products, but
such expansion is not possible within the limitations of the
company's own financial resources. In many cases, banks
and finance houses will be able to help with a loan. Where
this possibility is not suitable, another technique is to
raise money by public subscription. This involves letting
people have a share in the company in exchange for the
payment of a sum of money. Thus, a man who owns a
business may offer his three friends a quarter share in the
business if they each pay him £1000. In large enterprises,
the ownership of the company may be split into hundreds
or thousands of parts. When this is the case, it is more
convenient to consider the company divided into a specified number of *shares* each of £1 (or some other value).
This amount, £1 or whatever it is, is purely nominal and
it should not be thought that the share is worth this
amount. In the case of our man who shares his business
with his three friends, another method of expressing his
action would be to say that the company is to be regarded
as made up of 4000 shares each of £1. The owner proposes
to retain a thousand shares for himself and to sell the
remainder to his friends at the nominal value. Once a man
allows part of the ownership of his business to pass into
the hands of other people, the running of his business
becomes subject to legal rules concerning the proper
conduct of such companies.

Usually, a company does not obtain money from
friends but by offering its shares for sale to the public
through the Stock Exchange. By doing so, of course, it
has no control over the sort of people who will buy the
shares and they will thus be able to influence the conduct
of the company (through the legal rights which they
obtain by the purchase of the shares).

Before a company can put its shares up for sale in the

Stock Exchange, its activities are thoroughly investigated to see that the shares are being offered to the public at reasonable prices. But the subsequent behaviour of the company is a matter over which the Stock Exchange does not and could not exert control. Once a company has 'gone public' it may from time to time wish to raise further amounts of money by the sale of extra shares, which again requires investigation and approval from the Stock Exchange.

Shares we have so far considered are more precisely called *ordinary shares* or *deferred shares* and the people who buy these shares become ordinary shareholders and are, in effect, the owners of the business. Each year, the profit made by the company may, in part at least, be divided amongst the shareholders. This shared out profit is the *dividend*. In contrast to ordinary shares, *preference shares* have a prior claim on any profits the company may earn but they pay only a fixed rate of dividend. *Stock* is a word used to refer to shares which are brought and sold in fractional amounts rather than in whole numbers of shares. *Debentures* are fixed interest loans which a company may raise through the Stock Exchange, but in this case, no question of ownership of the company is involved.

In addition to the shares and debentures of companies, the Stock Exchange also deals in Government loans and local authority loans at fixed rates of interest. Loans issued by British and Commonwealth authorities are known as *gilt-edged* investments. To avoid confusion we shall confine our description to company shares, although it must be borne in mind that raising loans through the Stock Exchange is a most important method by which governments obtain money to finance their activities.

When a company obtains money by the sale of its shares, it then uses the money to buy buildings and

E

equipment in order to proceed with its projected line of business. But what if a shareholder suddenly needs his money back? Clearly he cannot get it from the company, since the money has been spent. He may however be able to find another person who is prepared to buy his shares for an agreed price. If so, his problem is solved and most of the procedure to be described below is avoided. But the seller will not, in general, be able to find a buyer from among his personal acquaintances. In this case he must turn to the Stock Exchange which will readily effect a sale for him. It is this assurance of being able to sell a share when the need of money arises, that enables the private citizen to invest in a company with confidence.

The Early Stockjobber

Like so many famous British institutions, the Stock Exchange was not suddenly created but developed stage by stage.

The need for a market for shares and loans arose in the seventeenth century because both Government and a number of trading enterprises wanted to raise money by borrowing it from the public. Stocks and shares were issued and these were bought and sold on an ever-increasing scale until people, known as 'stockjobbers', began to make a living by bringing together buyers and sellers. Thus, a regular market was formed.

During the latter half of the century, the stockjobbers established a meeting place in the old Royal Exchange. Later they moved and carried on their business in coffee houses around Change Alley. It was not long before the waiters in these coffee houses began to take messages and run errands, and so became an essential part of the dealings. For this reason, the attendants at the Stock Exchange are still called 'waiters'. In those days shares were issued by organizations engaged in foolhardy and questionable undertakings of a sort which the Stock Exchange would not countenance today.

One of the earliest companies offering shares to the public was the East India Company. Another was 'The Governor and Company of Adventurers of England Trading into Hudson's Bay', whose shares are bought and sold on the Stock Exchange to this day. Even in the early days, lists of stock prices were printed. One list issued for 25th January 1698 still exists. A note at the bottom indicates that the list was compiled by a dealer 'at his office at Jonathon's coffee house'.

In 1773, a building was taken over at the corner of Threadneedle Street and Sweetings Alley; over the door was inscribed a new title: 'The Stock Exchange'. The move to the present site was made in 1801.

The Stock Exchange of those early days was not the efficient reliable body that it is now, but through the years has come a full awareness of the responsibility which membership of this market entails. It is now governed by a Council of thirty-six members, a third of whom are elected in rotation every year by ballot. The regulations under which it works have been expanded and strengthened with the years so that the present rule book contains some 200 rules with numerous sub-sections and appendices. The aim of these rules, like that of the very strict unwritten code of behaviour which members observe, is to facilitate the transaction of business on the best and fairest terms and to provide maximum protection for both members and the investing public alike.

The Stock Exchange kept pace with the phenomenal expansion of Britain's industry in the nineteenth century. No longer the colourful assembly of the coffee-house days, it became a great public body which today serves efficiently as a free market for more than 9500 different shares and loans.

The present Stock Exchange was built in 1853 on the same site as the original building constructed in 1801. To keep pace with modern requirements and to provide the most up-to-date facilities both for members and investors, it has been decided once again to rebuild the Stock Exchange on the same site. Work started in 1966 and the new building will be completed in 1972.

Brokers and Jobbers

The present method of working in the Stock Exchange is necessitated by the large number of transactions brought together in one place. There are other ways in which this might be done but the system in use is considered to offer a most efficient free market in a wide range of shares.

The Stock Exchange is an association of some 3300 members who are divided into two groups: *brokers* and *jobbers*. Most members join together to form firms of brokers and firms of jobbers but this is for their own convenience and it does not bear directly on the working of the Exchange.

The jobber does not today deal directly with the public. He is essentially a wholesaler in a limited range of shares and he takes up a position on the floor of the Stock Exchange. By tradition, jobbers dealing in similar shares stand together on particular parts of the floor, e.g., oil shares, shipping shares, brewery shares. There are 515 jobbers divided among forty firms.

The brokers act as agents for the public in negotiating with the jobbers for the sale or purchase of shares. A member of the public, wishing to buy shares, starts by contacting a stockbroker who will advise him on an appropriate investment. When the buyer has decided on the particular company he wishes to invest in, he instructs the broker to buy for him a specified number of shares.

The approximate price will be known from newspaper reports, but the prices of shares are continually changing. The broker enters the Stock Exchange and approaches a jobber who is dealing in the shares. The broker asks the price but does not indicate at this stage if he desires to buy or sell. The jobber gives two prices: a buying price and a selling price, the latter being slightly higher. The difference between the two prices is known as the jobber's 'turn'. The broker then enquires similarly of other jobbers dealing in the same share. All jobbers will not have the same prices because a jobber with a lot of shares to sell may be prepared to accept a lower price than a jobber who has few of this particular share. The broker picks the jobber offering the lowest price and arranges to purchase the shares from him. This arrangement is effected by the broker and the jobber each making a note of the transaction in his book and the deal is done. No documents are signed, no written pledges are given. The deal made in this way is called a *bargain* and the method ensures that dealings can occur with the minimum of delay. On the other hand, it requires that jobbers and brokers are men of absolute integrity and honesty. Hence the Stock Exchange motto: 'My word is my bond'. From the moment when the broker and jobber make the deal, the shares are the property of the purchaser but a good deal of routine office work must follow before the purchaser gets his share certificate. In offering to deal in shares on the Stock Exchange, a jobber must be prepared to buy from or sell to a broker, shares to the value of £1000.

In return for his services, the broker charges the purchaser a fee. This fee depends on the type of share but is usually in the region of one per cent of the price of the shares. The jobber makes his money from the difference between the buying and selling prices of the shares. His profit is not automatic, however, because the prices of shares are continually changing and if prices were to fall suddenly, the jobber could lose. It is the competition between jobbers for the business of the brokers which establishes the 'market price' of each share and which causes these prices to fluctuate with the passage of time.

Dealings on the Stock Exchange take place in the morning and the afternoon. The end of the day is indicated by the sound of rattles. These sounds occur at 3.15 p.m. indicating that members can smoke and at 3.30 p.m. indicating the closing of the Exchange. Deals between jobbers and brokers may continue after hours by messenger or telephone.

On the day of the purchase, the broker sends the purchaser a *contract note* indicating the details of the bargain. In addition to the price of the shares and the broker's fee the purchaser must also pay taxes referred to as *transfer stamp* and *contract stamp* which together are in the region of one per cent of the purchase price of the shares. A small *registration fee* may be charged by the company whose shares are being bought. The contract note also states the *date of settlement* which is the date by which the purchaser must pay the broker. From the books of jobbers and brokers, checking sheets are prepared each day and clerks attend at the Checking Room of the Stock Exchange next morning to check that bargains have been correctly noted.

To inform the company, whose shares are being bought, the broker fills in a *transfer form* and sends it to the company. As a result of this, the company sends the purchaser a share certificate. The purchaser, if he wishes, can sell his shares again without awaiting the arrival of the certificate.

For a member of the public to sell shares, he must also contact a broker and the procedure is similar to that for a purchase. The broker enters the Stock Exchange and sells to the jobber offering him the highest price. A contract note is sent to the seller who is expected to hand over his share certificate and to sign the transfer form, which will authorize the company to remove his name from its records so that the buyer can in turn be registered.

Investors often form clubs to help and advise people on the buying and selling of shares. A logical extension of this club idea is the *unit trust* which is essentially a professionally operated investors' club. The managers look after the investing of the members' money in company shares and the members are issued with *units* which are effectively shares in the trust. The member is saved the trouble of going through the procedure of buying and selling shares himself. To buy units it is only necessary to fill in a form and send the money through the post. The member can sell his units back to the trust at any time at the prevailing price. The price of a unit fluctuates in relation to the prices of the shares owned by the trust.

There is no formal apprenticeship and there are no specific examinations for those wishing to be employed by firms of brokers and jobbers. Most firms recruit new entrants at about 16 to 18 years of age but many are taken on as university graduates. The new entrant is usually employed in general office work. Later he may have the opportunity of acting as an *unauthorized clerk*. In this position he is allowed on to the trading floor where his duties are mainly collecting prices from the jobbers and carrying messages. After two years and provided he is 21, he may become an *authorized clerk*, in which position he is allowed to deal on his firm's behalf. A candidate for membership of the Stock Exchange must have completed three years' training in a firm and must be at least 21. The annual membership fee exceeds £250. A career on the Stock Exchange is helped by an instinct or flair for this rather special type of business and an ability to make quick decisions and rapid calculations.

The Stock Exchange is an indispensable part of the City of London, which remains one of the greatest monetary centres in the world. Its financial and commercial interests extend to every country. Business from every continent is transacted on the floor of the London Stock Exchange. The tremendous industrial development which has been financed by public investment has ushered in the age of mass production. This has meant that it has been possible to bring a far greater variety of goods and services than ever before to the general public and standards of living are higher than our ancestors could have thought possible. The Stock Exchange, therefore, plays a vital part in all our lives. There is nothing mysterious about its function or the way it works. It is simply a market dealing in shares, which has grown and developed to provide a service. So long as Britain is a country in which people may set out to be their own masters and in which they may earn, save and invest their savings, the Stock Exchange will remain a vital factor in the nation's economy.

Investment and Gambling

Having outlined the working of the Stock Exchange, we shall now digress briefly to consider the motivations for the purchase of shares by the individual member of the public. Of course, the main result of the purchase of shares is the financing of industry and this remains true no matter what are the motives of the investor.

Investment through the Stock Exchange, for the individual investor, is essentially a rich man's game. This is because, for the small saver, other types of investment offer advantages. For the very small saver, important features are the safety and ready availability of the money.

Government savings facilities, offering these features, include the Post Office Savings Bank (for availability) and National Savings Certificates (for a good tax-free interest rate), both of which are as safe as investment can be. These methods of saving suffer from the fact that the money invested loses value due to inflation but for the very small saver this is not a serious consideration. For the intermediate saver, protection from inflation becomes important and this can be provided by investing in home ownership. The purchase of a house, as a long term investment, is likely to outmatch any other because of taxation advantages, particularly regarding capital gains tax. Thus it is the man with a large house and some Government investments, and who still has money to spare, who can profitably consider the Stock Exchange. Of Britain's fifty million inhabitants about $2\frac{1}{2}$ million have Stock Exchange investments. Many more contribute indirectly through life assurance policies and pension schemes.

For investment through the Stock Exchange, the investor has first to consider the degree of safety required. A range of Government loans are available offering fixed interest rates with complete security. Investment in the shares of companies always involves some risk but this may be thought worthwhile in order to reap a higher return. The risk arises from the danger of the company failing through bad management or through the company's products going out of fashion. The investor must also take into account whether he is interested in spending the proceeds of his investment or in continuous accumulation. The man saving for his retirement is not concerned with current interest yields but with the future prospects of the company in which he is investing. When he retires, however, his outlook changes and he wishes to reinvest his savings so as to provide a steady income from the highest current interest rates. Thus it is that the different types of share attract buyers. There is no shortage of shares to choose from. On the London Stock Exchange over 9500 different shares and loans are available having a total value of £82,000,000,000 which includes £20,000,000,000 of British Government Stock.

The reason why shares are considered to be good investments is that apart from the annual dividend, the prices of shares tend to rise with the passage of time. The underlying cause of this rise is the same as that for the rise in the price of houses. The permanent assets of a company, such as land, buildings and machinery, tend to increase in value due to the processes of inflation.

Each year, it is the duty of the directors of a company to decide how much of the profit will be used to improve and expand the company and how much will be given to the shareholders as dividend. If most of the profit is used for improvement, this increases the future prospects of the company. As we have seen, there are buyers for shares of companies no matter what the policy of the directors is in this respect.

Although the shares of well-established companies have a long term tendency to rise in price, the short term picture is very different. The day-to-day changes in prices of shares are the result of the sentiments of investors which may be rational or irrational as is the case with all other human behaviour. Good news for a company will tend to make its share price rise while bad news for the country as a whole may cause the prices of all shares to fall. In times of prosperity, prices rise in anticipation of larger profits, whereas in times of economic uncertainty, investors rush to get their money into safe investments, so that company shares fall in price. These are merely some of the influences on share prices, all of which and many others may act at the same time.

The result is that the short term variation in share prices has so far defied prediction.

A poor man could not get rich by investing through the Stock Exchange. It is possible, however, that he could do so by gambling on the Stock Exchange. His chances of doing so, though, are no greater than by any other form of gambling. Gambling consists of anticipating the peaks and troughs in the short-term variations in the price of a share. The gambler then buys shares at the troughs and sells at the peaks. A lucky run on half a dozen different shares could produce a small fortune. The great difficulty is that events in any part of the world may suddenly upset the best of calculations. An assassination or an international crisis can cause panic selling and a drop in prices which might not be recovered for months.

Newspaper and radio accounts of stock market activities sometimes contain traditional expressions such as 'bulls' and 'bears', which may be puzzling. In Stock Exchange phraseology a 'bull' is an individual who buys a share hoping that it will rise in value, while a 'bear' is a person who sells a share believing that prices will fall.

Thus a 'bull' market describes a state of financial confidence and rising prices, while a 'bear' market means that the economic trend is uncertain and values are expected to fall.

A final point must be made, which is conveniently overlooked by most investors. A shareholder, as part owner of a company, is directly responsible for all that goes on in the company. Thus, to invest for maximum profit, regardless of the methods by which this profit is made, is just as morally reprehensible as the misdeeds in the investor's own activities.

Computer Applications

The amount of clerical work arising from the activities of
the Stock Exchange is enormous and much of it can be
transferred to a computer. One day, a giant computer
may replace the trading floor of the Exchange but this
possibility is not in sight at the present time. In this
section, we shall consider briefly how computers are
already being applied to Stock Exchange and investment
activities.

Firms of jobbers make use of computers in their
accounting work. Each day the details of bargains, which
are recorded in the jobbers' books, are punched into cards
for input to the computer. Each share in which the jobber
deals is given a code number and each broker also has an
identification number. Thus each bargain is specified by
five items of information: the identification number of
the broker with whom the bargain has been made; the
code number of the share involved; the number of shares;
the price; and whether bought or sold. Each evening, the
cards are read into the computer and the information is
stored on a magnetic file. The computer prints out the
checking sheets needed by the firm's clerks for checking
the day's business. Any discrepancy in the information is
corrected by punching further cards which are read into
the computer on the following day. Also each day, other
information may be printed by the computer, including
total numbers of each share bought and sold and whether
a profit or loss has been made. Traditionally, dealings on
the Stock Exchange are divided into accounting periods
of two weeks. At the end of each such period, summary
information is printed by the computer.

Private investors, and people concerned with the investment of money for insurance companies and other organizations, are anxious to be well informed on the affairs

of companies in which they invest. For many years, books have been published which devote a page or two to each of the most important shares on the market and give details of dividends and share price movements in previous years. By storing such information in a computer, and by continually updating it, the investor can have access to information on the latest trends. This is done by means of a keyboard and printer, combined together so as to have the appearance of a typewriter. Such devices can be installed in the offices of people requiring the service, for an annual fee, and are connected by cable to the computer centre which may be some distance away. At the centre, daily share prices and other information are fed into the computer on punched cards, so as to keep the stored information up to date. In the office of the customer, a person can tap the computer-stored information by indicating the particular company in which he is interested. This is done by pressing the keys of the keyboard in an appropriate manner. The keyboard is connected by cable directly to the computer and as a result of the message sent to it in this way, the computer causes the desired information to be sent back through the cable for output by the printer in the customer's office. A most important item of information about a share, in which investors are interested, is the *price-to-earnings ratio*. This is effectively the rate of interest on the share. It is calculated from the current share price and the last annual dividend. This is a calculation which can easily be performed by a computer. By an appropriate keyboard instruction, the computer can be made to do the calculation and print the result in the customer's office. Another useful calculation which the computer can be made to do is *portfolio valuation*. When a person, or organization, holds a variety of shares, his collection is often referred to as his 'portfolio'. As the prices of shares fluctuate with the passage of time, it is naturally of interest to the investor to know how the total value of his portfolio is getting on. By keying details of the portfolio (i.e., number of each share) into the computer, it will calculate the total value, based on current share prices, and cause this value to be printed in the customer's office. Computers used for this type of work do not use magnetic tapes for storage purposes as all information must be readily available. This necessitates the use of magnetic discs as the means of storage. The keyboard and printer technique of tapping computer-stored information is finding applications in the dissemination of all kinds of facts which may be of interest to businessmen.

Computers are being applied to the accounting work which arises in the running of unit trusts.

Share Registration

It will now be appreciated that in many companies there is the important office job of maintaining a list of names of company shareholders and their addresses so that dividends can be sent to them. This task is ideally suited to the computer, which can hold the list in a magnetic file and this can be amended by punched card input. The computer can print dividend warrants; it can also print new share certificates whenever shares change hands.

8 Local and Central Government

In our consideration of the business world, we have so far been almost entirely concerned with private enterprise. We must now turn and look at the uses of computers in the administration of the country as a whole.

Local Government

The United Kingdom is divided for administrative purposes into about 1400 *local authority* areas. These local authorities are responsible for the day-to-day administration of many of the policies of the Government, particularly where they relate to local conditions. This gives rise to clerical work which can be to a considerable extent taken over by computers. The computer techniques are the same as we have already considered for private enterprise, and it is necessary only for us to mention those aspects of local authority work where computers are currently finding application. Most local authorities are of a size which justifies the use of the smaller types of computer.

Apart from the overall accounting for the local authority, the computer can help by printing dividend warrants for the interest on loans which the authority raises to help in financing its work.

The work of the local authority can be conveniently divided into departments, each of which can be run exactly like a company with its own payroll, stores and accounting. There are departments for education, public libraries and road maintenance. There is the housing department which is concerned with the maintenance and rent collecting for the increasing number of homes owned by local authorities. Some local authorities also act like building societies and offer loans to home buyers. Some authorities also deal with the water supply and run the local bus service.

Of course, there are other sides to local authority work besides the purely commercial aspects we have mentioned above. As far as computers are concerned, however, it remains for us to consider a few activities which have no equivalent in company administration.

Some local authorities are considering the computer storing of school health records. Such storing will enable statistics on various aspects of health and illness to be readily calculated. Such statistics attract a good deal of public attention, as apart from the natural interest of parents, these statistics are considered by many to indicate the general level of prosperity and progress of the community.

It is the duty of the local authority to produce each year an electoral register which is a printed list of the persons entitled to vote in elections. The register is arranged in order of streets and house numbers; the information for the register is obtained by requesting householders to fill in a form once per year. Since the register will largely remain unaltered from one year to the next, a computer scheme has been devised in which the register is maintained on a magnetic file. Only the annual modifications need then be punched into cards. The computer uses the cards to update the file and print out the up-to-date register ready to be sent to the printer. With the trend towards computer-controlled printing, it will eventually be possible to set up the print directly from the magnetic file holding the register information.

Local authorities raise much of the money they require by a tax on property called *rates*, and this gives rise to *rate accounting*. For the purpose of this tax, each property is given a *rateable value* which is arbitrarily fixed by the authority but is intended to increase with the desirability and grandeur of the property, be it private residence or business premises. Each year the rate of tax is fixed by the authority as so much in the £ of rateable value. Thus if the rate is fixed at £0·5 in the £, then a man owning a house which has a rateable value of £50 would have to pay rates to the value of £25. Due to inflation, the rate increases from year to year. To computerize rate accounting, a file is established of the properties in the area of the local authority. The record for each property includes its address, its owner and its rateable value. To calculate the amount of rates required from each property, it is necessary only to provide the computer with the proposed rate per £. The computer can then calculate the rates required by multiplying this figure by the rateable value of the property. Having performed this calculation, the computer can print the notice which must be sent to the owner telling him to pay up. The treatment of the resulting money can be computerized as for accounts receivable. Rate accounting is complicated by the fact that some owners require their notices sent to different addresses. Further, where a landlord owns several houses, he likes them all on the same notice. These difficulties can be handled by allocating more file storage space to such properties. A further difficulty occurs when a property changes hands and the rates must be split between the two owners.

In the above discussion of rate accounting, it will be seen that the file of properties is not altered by the annual rate calculation but, of course, it has to be amended due to such things as properties changing hands and new properties being erected. In these circumstances, a magnetic file of properties is not really necessary and instead the information can remain on punched cards. During the course of the year, these cards are maintained up to date just like an ordinary card index. When the time comes to perform the rate calculation, the cards are read into the computer in batches. Dispensing with magnetic tape in this way greatly reduces the cost of the computer and such schemes have a wide application in smaller businesses. Prior to computers, punched card systems existed which were processed by electromechanical equipment.

Local authority computers are used by their engineering departments for technical calculations connected with surveying and highway construction.

Central Government

The Government has been steadily purchasing computers for applications in its many and varied activities.

The administration and accounting for Government-operated saving schemes are now in process of being computerized. The same may be said of the collection of taxes, namely, income tax, national insurance and graduated pension scheme. The payment of pensions will also be administered with the aid of a computer.

Payroll and personnel records are being computerized for the vast number of Government employees, namely civil servants, police and the armed forces. In connection with police work, the computer storing of criminal records is also in progress.

Hospital accounting is receiving attention. Schemes to put records of patients on computer files are also under consideration, but to expect computers to contribute significantly to the progress of medicine would be hoping for too much.

Computers have been used for many years in Government scientific and research establishments, and they are now finding applications in operational equipment for the armed forces.

The nationalized industries are extensive users of computers. To mention only one example, the preparation of electricity and gas bills can be undertaken by computer. This involves the insertion of meter readings into the computer via punched cards, after which the computer can calculate the bill from the current charge per unit. This application has many similarities with rate accounting.

We shall conclude by mentioning a computer project of some complexity which is being undertaken for the Export Services Branch of the Board of Trade. The aim is to use a computer to sort and process the mass of information which passes through this department. It presently has a headquarters staff of 480 and in addition it has 1200 commercial officers attached to diplomatic posts throughout the world. The information flow is in two directions. It is the duty of the commercial officers to pass to London any report, hint or piece of intelligence which may be of interest to British exporters. In all, about 600,000 items of information are sent in each year and these must be sifted and passed on to appropriate British companies. In the other direction, some 2500 enquiries per day are received from British firms requiring agents abroad or advice on export possibilities. Also enquiries are received from foreign firms wishing to buy British goods. The Export Services Branch is the Government's contribution to the country's export drive, the success of which is essential to the prosperity of the nation.

9 Transport

Companies operating transport services have activities which we have considered in Chapters 2 to 4. In addition, there are clerical activities peculiar to transport which can be aided by a computer.

Airlines

A wasteful feature of present-day airline operation is the large number of different companies offering services over the same route. Each company produces a timetable and a firm in London produces the *ABC Airline Guide*, which includes timetables for every airline in the world. This guide was a convenient collection for the experienced traveller, but it gave little help to a person wishing to know what flights existed between London and New York, for example, on a Sunday afternoon. In order to make information of this type more readily available, the firm decided to add a quick reference section listing the flights between any pair of cities. This section was issued originally for European cities and was so successful that it was decided to make it world-wide. The task, however, was too great for human compilation and so a large computer was used for the purpose. The quick reference section now consists of the output from the computer with headings in conventional print. As the timetables change, it is necessary to revise this section periodically using the computer. The *ABC Airline Guide* consists of pages measuring eleven inches by eight. The timetable section is three-quarters of an inch thick and the quick reference section is one and a quarter inches thick.

Computers are in use in connection with the reservation of seats on flights. The computer is made to store information on every flight which an airline will offer from the current date until about a year ahead. For each flight, there must be sufficient storage space for details of the passenger who will occupy each seat. The computer is connected by cable to keyboard and printer units in the airline's reservation offices. Arrangements may also be made to connect the computer to such units at distant offices by Datel links. When an intending passenger enquires at a reservation office if a seat is available on a particular flight, the clerk can pass the question to the computer by pressing the keys of the keyboard in an appropriate manner. From the stored information, the computer sends the reply back and this is output on the printer. If the flight in question is already fully booked, the clerk can enquire if other flights on the same day have vacant seats. When a suitable seat has been found and the passenger has agreed to make the reservation, his details can be sent for storage in the computer by the same keyboard technique. Cancellations are similarly notified to the computer. This method is the only one by which reservation clerks can know the up-to-the-minute situation on all flights. It does require, however, that the computer be 100 per cent reliable over extensive periods of time.

The size of the undertaking for a large airline is indicated by the fact that ten million seats may be offered over a year and a thousand offices may be connected to the computer.

In this application, an alternative to the printer is a cathode-ray tube display. This is like a television screen upon which writing can be made to appear. This type of display is finding many other uses.

The computer can also be used to allocate seat numbers to passengers before they board the aircraft.

A widespread organization, like an airline, has occasion to send frequent telegraph messages between its various installations. Quite often one message has to be sent to several other stations. This *message switching* activity can be undertaken by a computer. The computer is situated at a central position in the network and all incoming messages are held temporarily in the computer store. As output channels become available, the messages are sent off to their destinations. Where the code in the message indicates more than one destination, the computer sends two or more separate messages to the necessary destinations. An airline application is the reporting of the progress of an aircraft which is destined to land at a number of places on its route. The technique also has applications in international business organizations and in news agencies concerned with the dissemination of stock exchange and commodity prices.

On the technical side of airline operation, computers are finding application in air traffic control. Small computers in the aircraft are used for navigation and in the automatic landing schemes at present being developed.

Hotel Reservations

Closely associated with air travel is the problem of hotel reservations. In the United States, a start has been made in putting hotel reservations on a computer basis using the technique developed for the airlines. Pan-American World Airways uses a flight reservation system through which bookings can be made at a limited range of hotels. The chain of Holiday Inns, comprising 850 hotels, has its own computerized reservation scheme.

Shipping

Reservations in shipping are not such a hectic matter as they are in airline operation and the computer has hardly been applied to them. One example does exist, however, and it is interesting in that the authorities were forced to use a computer by the pressure of events. The Danish State Railways operate 16 car ferries which together carry up to 20,000 cars per day. A space reservation system has been installed so that enquiries from 117 booking offices throughout Denmark, and a number of others in Germany, are transmitted to the computer situated in Copenhagen. The computer is linked to the booking offices by the railway's own telegraph network. The system handles a peak load of 4000 enquiries per hour. Bookings are accepted for up to two months ahead.

Throughout the world, the growing volume of motor vehicles has been accompanied by a host of new problems. A particular problem experienced in countries composed either wholly or partially of islands has been to provide adequate facilities for transporting ever-increasing numbers of vehicles by sea. Denmark consists of the Jutland peninsula and several hundred islands but it is so situated that its ferries form an important extension of the road network in linking Europe to Scandinavia. By 1957, peak traffic loads had necessitated the introduction of reservations and in that year a central control station was set up using electromechanical transmission equipment. Within a few years, however, the demand for reservations rose to a point at which this scheme was no longer adequate and a computer was installed in 1964.

Computers will be an important element in the dockland of the future. They will contribute to the efficient cargo handling arrangements which will be necessary with the changeover to container traffic. In the more immediate future, a computer will hold records of all cargo in the dock. This information will be fed to the computer by clerks at control points using keyboard and printer units which will also have cathode-ray tube displays. Details of imported cargo consignments, for example, will be held in the computer. As the arrival of new consignments from ships is notified, a clerk will type in the details, which will cause a new record to be set up in the computer store. As events occur which affect the status of the consignment, the clerk will type in the details to update the record. Such events are clearance by Customs and possible transfer of ownership. When a lorry arrives to collect all or part of the consignment, the clerk will key in a request to sight the record, which, within seconds, will be displayed on the cathode-ray tube. The clerk will then be able to check the driver's title to the goods, their shed location, that they have been cleared by Customs, and that the quantity to be collected is in fact on hand. When these checks are satisfied, the clerk will be able to request the computer to print out a delivery note which will be presented to the lorry driver as his authority to collect the goods.

A further application in the docks is the calculation of *demurrage*. This is a special rental scheme which has the effect of penalizing users who leave cargoes on the docks for more than a specified time. For the scheme to work efficiently, dock users must be informed immediately when charges are accruing; a task which the computer can, of course, carry out effectively.

The Port of Liverpool was the first port authority in Britain (and the fourth port in the world) to install a computer, in 1962, for general accounting work. Such work includes the calculation of pilotage dues. The computer is also used for technical calculations in connection with marine surveying.

At sea, equipment records such things as fuel consumption and engine operating conditions of a ship. These data are subsequently fed into a computer for statistical calculations. The resulting statistics are used by designers in their endeavour to produce more efficient engines and operating procedures.

A further application to shipping, though a technical one, deserves mention. It is the preparation of tide tables. At some ports, ships can only get into harbour at high water, so it is important to know in advance exactly when it will be. It is usual to make tide tables for a port giving the times and heights of high and low water for a whole year. Allowing time for printing and distribution, this means that the tide tables must be prepared at least two years in advance. Since 1964, computers have been used to work out the water heights and times. The movement of the sea is caused by the gravitational pull of the sun and moon upon it. Before 1964, water heights were obtained by using a complicated machine which indicated the sea movements by a pointer moving up and down a scale. A girl had to watch the pointer and copy down the height of the water. The written tables then went to the printer. When a computer is used, no human writing is involved. Tide tables are made by the Liverpool Tidal Institute at Bidston Hill. For 1968, tables have been made for 37 ports in Britain and 136 ports overseas.

Railways

On the Continent, railway rolling stock of one nationality may be run over the lines of several different countries. Charges are made for this. The French National Railways, in order to calculate its charges on foreign wagons entering its territories, has checkpoints at the frontiers. From these points, information on all movements in and out of the country is sent via data transmission facilities to the computer centre in Paris. Here, a computer digests the information and creates records for wagons entering the system. For wagons leaving the system, its record is located and from the times and positions of entering and leaving, the appropriate charge can be worked out and deducted from an account for the foreign railway concerned. The technique has also been used to make statistical checks on French wagons. These have revealed the painful fact that on the average, a freight wagon is moving for only one day out of every six, the rest of the time being spent in sidings.

10 Miscellaneous Applications

In this chapter we collect together a few topics which could not be conveniently dealt with earlier.

Almost all the applications of computers we have so far considered, and those of the present chapter as far as the section on bets, consist essentially of the input, output and storing of information in the form of records together with a modest amount of arithmetic. There are a few business applications of computers which involve geometrical and mathematical considerations and we shall consider these in the remaining sections of the book.

Computerized House Selling

This is not a field of business where computers are likely to be a success. The traditional method of selling houses is to make use of the services of an estate agent, though not all sellers do this. The estate agent advertises the house in the local newspaper and when a sale is effected, the estate agent receives a percentage of the selling price from the seller in payment.

Two computer schemes have been proposed. One is intended to bypass the agent and bring the buyer and seller into direct contact. The idea is that countrywide records of houses for sale be maintained on a magnetic file. For a small charge per month, a seller can have his property entered on the file. Details recorded include price asked, number of rooms, bathrooms, type of property (e.g., detached, semi, flat or bungalow), location (e.g., town, suburb, village or country), proximity to shops, services available (e.g., gas, electricity). Also recorded is the county or town where the house is situated. For a small charge a buyer can have the computer print out a dozen or so houses in the position and price range which he requires. If a sale is effected, no further payment is made to the firm operating the computer.

The snag about this scheme is that a buyer can see all the houses available in the area, at no charge, merely by looking in the local paper. Also, the estate agent can often help the buyer with mortgage and legal arrangements without charge.

The second scheme is essentially the same as far as the computer is concerned but involves the active co-operation of the estate agents. The point of the scheme is to provide information for people moving to distant areas. Statistics show, however, that only 10 per cent of moves are more than 35 miles. Local advertising is thus sufficient to attract the great majority of custom. Further, leading agents report that for every ten enquiries received from another part of the country, about eight are personal callers. In short, agents do not believe that the use of computers can gain them any more business than the existing and cheaper methods of promotion.

Instant Tickets

A scheme similar to that for airline reservations has been installed in Los Angeles for the purpose of issuing tickets for various forms of entertainment, such as theatres and sporting events. The computer will initially be connected to terminals in 52 supermarkets. The computer will store information relating to prices and location of about ten million seats for as many as 800 different entertainment events. The terminals, in addition to transmitting information to and from the computer, will also print tickets. Upon a customer requesting reservations, the sales clerk uses the terminal to enquire if the desired seats are available. If not, the computer offers the next best. For this, the seats at a given price are stored in the computer in an 'order of desirability'. When the customer agrees to purchase, the tickets are issued and the computer-stored information is modified accordingly.

Information Systems

Here we mention some further examples of the application of the keyboard and printer technique of tapping computer-stored information.

The Los Angeles Retail Merchants Credit Association provides such keyboard units in its members' shops so that the credit worthiness of customers can be checked before goods are sold on credit.

Complete specifications of the 40,000 merchant ships listed by Lloyd's Register of Shipping have been stored in a computer. Using keyboard units, lists of ships can be produced having specified characteristics.

In New York, Law Research Services Inc. is using a computer to provide a service which enables lawyers to obtain instant references to precedents relating to cases which they are preparing. The area of the law involved is specified by a keyboard code. The computer, in reply, causes the printing of relevant case details including name of state, names of individuals concerned and the volume and page number of the legal document where the information appears.

An alternative scheme for tapping computer-stored information is to 'phone' the computer. For this purpose, a telephone is situated in the office of the customer and is connected to the computer, instead of a keyboard. When the receiver is lifted, the caller is in contact with the computer. He conveys his enquiry by dialling a code number. The computer then speaks back the required information. This is effected by having the sounds of individual words recorded on a magnetic store similar to a tape recorder. According to its stored information, the computer causes the appropriate words to be selected to form the answer and the appropriate sounds are transmitted to the caller. Such a scheme is used in the United States by a telephone company to tell long-distance operators the cost of calls. The system handles 5000 enquiries per hour from operators throughout a five-state region. Formerly, it took operators using a rate book 45 seconds or longer to determine the cost.

The keyboard method of conveying business information may not always be justified if the number of enquiries made per week is low. In such circumstances, it may be more convenient to convey the information by means of a computer printout sent periodically through the post. An example is the storage in a computer of information on new electronic equipment, the information being continually updated. Subscribers can specify the type of equipment in which they are interested and this specification for each subscriber is also stored in the computer. At weekly or monthly intervals, the computer prints out an information sheet for each subscriber giving him latest information on the equipment he is concerned with. The method is clearly applicable to all kinds of business information and is also being used to disseminate scientific and library information.

Media Planning

Advertising agencies are using computers to help in planning advertising campaigns. Such campaigns involve placing advertisements in newspapers, magazines and on posters. The selection of these 'media' depends on the type of person the advertisement is intended to attract,

By storing a list of available media and the types of people which are likely to see them, a computer can help to produce the best campaign for a given expenditure.

Bets

A racing association uses a computer in conjunction with ticket issuing machines to record all bets and to compute odds and pay-offs instantaneously.

Responsive Stock Control

In Chapter 3, we saw how a computer can handle records of the amounts of stock in a company's store and can arrange the ordering of replacement stock. For this purpose, two numbers are held in the record, namely, the re-order level and the re-order quantity. The computer arranges for a replacement order to be sent to the supplier when the stock of a commodity falls below the re-order level. The re-order quantity is the quantity involved in the replacement order. These two numbers are fixed as far as the computer is concerned, their values having been decided beforehand by the management in the light of previous experience.

In the wholesale and retail trades, efficient stock control contributes significantly to the profitability of the business because such a large amount of the company's money is tied up in stock. If stocks are allowed to fall too low, customers cannot be satisfied and so trade, and hence profit, is lost. On the other hand, if stocks are allowed to build up unduly, too much of the company's money is immobilized unnecessarily and there is the danger that the commodities may go out of fashion.

These considerations determine the re-order level which the management decides upon. The re-order quantity depends on the re-order level and the behaviour of the supplier. If the supplier is reliable and can deliver

quickly, then the re-order quantity can be small. On the
other hand, if the supplier cannot deliver quickly, it is
necessary to ask for a large quantity to cover the uncertainty of the delivery date. Re-order quantities may

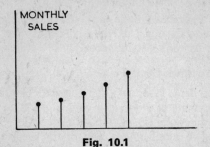

Fig. 10.1

also be affected by transport changes, which are often
cheaper for large deliveries and by the fact that the
supplier may offer discounts on large orders.

So much for the considerations which apply to stock
control for commodities which are of a traditional nature

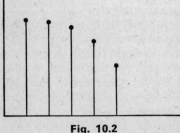

Fig. 10.2

and which sell steadily year after year. On the other hand,
for commodities subject to fashion, the matter becomes
more complicated. Suppose in Fig. 10.1 that the heights

of the dots represent the sales of a commodity in successive months of the year. It is tempting to assume that in the months immediately ahead, sales will continue to rise and that stocks should be increased in anticipation. In Fig. 10.2 the indication is that a previously popular item is suddenly losing favour, possibly due to competition from a new firm. In these circumstances it would be advisable to consider a price reduction or if this is not feasible, then to run down stocks.

Seldom, however, are trends as clearly defined as this. Quite frequently a long term trend is masked by seasonal variations. Large but infrequent individual orders may also upset the month-to-month sales figures. But if the computer could be made to assess the trends in sales, it could alter the re-order level and re-order quantity from month to month to ensure that stocks are always at the ideal level.

The computer manufacturers claim that their computers can be made to do this and they provide programmes for the purpose. They involve the use of sophisticated mathematical and statistical techniques.

Economic Planning

Attempts to use computers for economic forecasting and planning on a scale larger than the individual company have so far met only with failure. This has not been due to any inability of the computer to perform the calculations. It has resulted from the fact that market conditions are so complex and dependent on so many factors that nobody has yet succeeded in specifying the calculations which the computer should undertake. The science of economics is at present limited to a study of simplified concepts which, though important in giving a general understanding of business trends, are totally inadequate for detailed forecasting.

F

Delivery Routing

In Chapter 4, we saw how the need arises for a computer method to select routes for vehicles engaged in the delivery of a company's products. Given a number of points on the map, the ways in which they can be joined together to form a string are considerable. Three points can be joined to make three possible routes. Four points can be joined to make twelve possible routes. Five points can be joined to make sixty possible routes. The number of possible routes climbs very steeply as the number of points increases. We are, of course, interested in a route which is reasonably direct so that the mileage can be kept to a minimum. We also saw in Chapter 4 that the number of points on one journey is limited by the total load which the vehicle can carry.

The obvious approach is for the computer to work out the distance covered on every possible route and select the route which involves the minimum distance. Unfortunately, the number of possible routes is so great in practical delivery problems that this method is just not feasible. Even at the electronic speeds at which a computer can perform calculations, it would still take hours to decide the best route. This being so, some other method has to be devised, which produces reasonable journeys, though not necessarily the best possible.

One method, suitable for a computer, starts from the most inefficient route structure and endeavours to improve upon it. The most inefficient routing involves a separate journey from the depot to each customer and back. Let us improve on this by joining two points together on just one journey, the remaining journeys still involving one customer only. How can the two points be chosen so as to produce the most saving? Let us suppose there are 100 delivery points. A pair of these points can be chosen in just under 5000 ways. A computer could run through these possibilities in a short amount of time and select the pair which involves the greatest saving of mileage. Let the points chosen be called A and B. They are taken as the basis for our first string. The next problem is to choose a point C so that by including it with A and B on a journey we obtained the greatest saving of mileage. As there are 98 points left, it follows that there are 98 possibilities for C. The computer can quickly run through these and select the best. It has to decide also if C should be joined to A or to B to produce the best route. Having found C, the computer next selects point D from the remaining 97 possibilities to extend the string to four points. The process continues until the load is sufficient for one vehicle. The selection process then starts afresh for the remaining delivery points: the best pair are found and the string is extended until another sufficient load has been accumulated. In this way, strings are formed until all delivery points have been dealt with. The effect of this method is to join up the most outlying points first and then to work inwards. This is in contrast to the method used by most human planners, which involves grouping together customers in districts.

In performing the calculations, the computer uses two numbers for each delivery point. These are the distances, measured north and east, of the delivery point from the depot. From these numbers, the straight-line distances from depot to delivery points and between delivery points can be worked out. It is true that the vehicle cannot follow these straight lines as the roads will not always lie along them. However, the inaccuracy resulting from this will be much the same for most of the possible routes.

Some operators claim that computer routing reduces delivery costs but this may be too much to hope for in general. Routes will never be strictly adhered to.

Frequently a detour will be made to avoid heavy traffic or to visit a favourite café. A further complication arises when empty containers have to be returned in the same vehicle, which may involve backtracking or an extra journey.

Computer Graphics

A computer can be made to draw pictures on paper. When a pencil is used to draw in the usual way, at any instant of time the pencil will be at a definite point on the paper. This point can be specified by two numbers: one measuring the distance of the point from the left edge of the paper and one measuring the distance of the point from the bottom of the paper. Mechanical equipment exists which can cause a pen to move over a sheet of paper, provided it is given these two numbers at each instant of time. A computer can be programmed to provide the pairs of numbers and so any desired pattern can be drawn on the paper.

This technique has been used for some years for scientific purposes and it has recently found applications in business. One firm is using a computer to produce graphs of the behaviour of share prices and other Stock Exchange information over the course of a year.

11 Project Planning

In this final chapter we shall consider a technique which can aid management in the planning of projects. By *project*, we mean any human endeavour directed towards a specific objective. Usually, the projects to which this technique is applied are large and complex construction jobs.

Let us start by considering a project to which many people will have applied themselves: the establishment of a garden for a new house. For this project, we can distinguish five distinct phases of the work. These phases are as follows. The numbering will be explained below.

(1–2) clear ground
(2–3) prepare surface
(1–3) purchase seeds and plants
(3–4) plant seeds and plants
(4–5) control weeds

Having recognized the tasks to be performed, the next question is whether they must be done in any particular order. Clearing the ground must obviously precede preparing the surface, which must precede planting, which must precede weed control. On the other hand, purchase of the seeds and plants can take place at any time before planting. It can thus be the first, second or third activity, or it can be undertaken by a second person while the first is clearing the ground and preparing the surface. This relationship between the tasks is clearly indicated by

means of a *network diagram*. Such a diagram for our
project is shown in Fig. 11.1. The tasks are represented
by arrows and a particular arrow is identified by the
numbers in the circles at its tip and tail. This explains the
numbering of the tasks in the list above. The diagram
indicates that tasks (1–2) and (2–3) can take place inde-
pendently of task (1–3) but that all these tasks must be
completed before task (3–4) can be commenced.

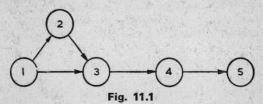

Fig. 11.1

With this simple example in mind, we can now proceed
to consider the general principles involved in establishing
a network for a project. First the project is given a name
and the objective is concisely stated. A list is then made of
the tasks involved in achieving the objective, this list
being known as the *work breakdown schedule*. The
network diagram for the project is constructed from these
tasks, due regard being given to the order in which they
are to be performed.

Network Principles

The network is made up of two symbols: an arrow to
represent an *activity* and a circle to represent an *event*.
Numbering the circles provides a method of identifying
both the events and the activities. In order for this method
of identifying arrows to be effective, it is necessary that
there should not be more than one arrow between any
pair of events. Subject to this restriction, the arrows can
be bent, if this improves the clarity of the diagram.

An activity is a task of work and requires human effort. It may also require material resources, machinery and equipment. It requires time for its completion and usually it costs money.

An event is a specific accomplishment that occurs at a recognizable point in time. The event occurs when all the activities are completed, which are represented by arrows pointing to the circle. An event does not itself involve human labour, resources or cost. Activities represented by arrows, whose tails are attached to the circle, cannot be started until the event occurs. Two events in the network are of particular interest. They are the *network-beginning event* usually denoted by circle 1 and the *network-ending event* which marks the completion of the project.

Using these two symbols a network can be produced for any project, however complex. The construction of networks for such projects is not easy and requires much care, experience and effort.

As a further example of network construction let us consider the tasks involved in building a conventional house. Our scheme may not conform with best building practice but it will nonetheless serve our purpose. In building a house, the ground must first be cleared of any trees or bushes. Foundation trenches can then be dug and the foundations built up to floor level. Two independent tasks follow: concreting of the floor and building of the walls. When the walls are complete, three tasks can follow: building the chimney; fitting doors and windows; building the roof. The interior woodwork can be undertaken when the floor has been concreted and the roof is complete. Upon completion of the interior woodwork and also the fitting of the doors and windows, two further independent tasks can commence: the painting of the interior woodwork and the plastering of the walls.

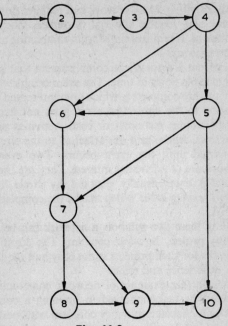

Fig. 11.2

Distempering follows plastering. When painting and distempering are complete, the thermoplastic floor covering is laid.

Fig. 11.2 is the network for this project where the activities are as follows:

(1–2)	clear ground	1·0
(2–3)	dig trenches	1·0
(3–4)	build foundations	1·0
(4–5)	build walls	4·0
(4–6)	concrete floor	1·0
(5–6)	build roof	2·0

(5–7)	fit doors and windows	4·0
(5–10)	build chimney	1·0
(6–7)	interior woodwork	1·0
(7–8)	plaster	0·5
(7–9)	paint	2·0
(8–9)	distemper	0·5
(9–10)	cover floor	1·0

The figures on the right will be referred to later in the chapter.

A particular network diagram can be drawn in a variety of ways by placing the event circles at different positions on the paper. This feature is useful as it enables complicated networks to be drawn in such a manner that activities of a particular type lie within a given area of the paper, e.g., areas may be allocated to design, drawing office, workshop, assembly.

PERT

Although the network technique appears simple in concept, it may surprise the reader to learn that it did not become generally known until the late 1950s when it was used by the U.S. Navy Special Projects Office in connection with the Polaris project. Prior to this, a variety of graphical representations were in use to help the planner, but none had the advantages of the network technique. The Navy scheme, based on the network diagram, was called Program Evaluation and Review Technique, or PERT.

The circumstances of the Polaris project, although occurring in peacetime, necessitated a wartime approach to the problem. Soviet space and missile achievements had left the United States sadly behind in the nuclear arms race. The Polaris system, by which missiles could be fired from submerged submarines, was seen as a means of rapidly redressing the balance of power. This was because at the time there was no means of detecting submarines resting beneath the surface, so a few such submarines, capable of firing missiles at any part of Russia, would be sufficient to deter the Russians from surprise aggression. It was decided that such a submarine system would be put into service as quickly as possible and to this end all necessary scientific and manufacturing resources of the country would be committed. The technical and engineering problems were substantial but even more so were the problems of overall co-ordination.

To give some idea of the vastness of the problem, a method had to be found by which those in charge of the Polaris project could deal with 250 prime contractors and at least 9000 subcontractors. These numbers may not at first appear to represent such a staggering task until one realizes that the failure of any one of the subcontractors to deliver one small, seemingly insignificant component might slow up or even stall the entire project. Then when one considers the enormous number of possibilities for this type of delay, the problem assumes a magnitude which overshadows even the development of the first atomic weapon.

A method had to be developed which would allow the management of the Polaris project to co-ordinate the efforts of all these firms, to anticipate the occurrence of bottlenecks, to forecast with reasonable certainty the extent to which target dates would be met and in general to channel the efforts of literally hundreds of thousands of persons into a finished operational weapon. PERT was the solution. The Navy Department has stated on several occasions that because of the use of PERT, the Polaris missile submarine was brought to combat readiness about two full years ahead of the original date scheduled.

In the remaining sections of this chapter we shall

consider further aspects of the PERT method. Since this initial application of the method, it has been elaborated and developed. No longer is PERT mainly identified with and used by the military. Manufacturers, builders and advertising agencies are types of commercial firms that use the tool. It is used in research and development, in construction, in the launching of new products and in various marketing activities. Recently a stadium was built in Atlanta for major-league baseball and football. Construction time was held to less than twelve months through the use of the critical path method, a variant of PERT.

Today PERT is both forcing and permitting managers to think each major programme and project through in its entirety and in detail. It identifies possible delays for managers and it aids in resolving the difficulties. It helps managers make earlier deadlines because of continuous, effective control. PERT contributes to the optimum utilization of resources, particularly money, time and manpower.

Zero-Time Activities

In the construction of networks, circumstances can arise where the use of a dummy activity is necessary. This is because we have excluded the possibility of two arrows passing between a given pair of events. This exclusion was necessitated by our system of numbering to identify the arrows.

In the construction of a bridge across a river, the initial stages of building on the left bank and right bank are independent. When this building is ready on both sides, the central section can be fitted to complete the bridge. Fig. 11.3 shows a network to represent the bridge construction. The left bank building is (1–2) and the right bank building is (1–3). But the fitting of the central

section (3–4) can only take place when both (1–2) and
(1–3) are finished. We complete the network with a
zero-time activity, represented by the dotted arrow. This
dummy activity requires no time for its execution and
costs nothing. Its use in the diagram, however, enables
the relationships between the other activities to be
properly represented.

Fig. 11.3 illustrates an important point about network
diagrams. The degree of detail which the planner chooses
to include in his diagram depends entirely on his requirements. For a bridge, we might expect that, in actual

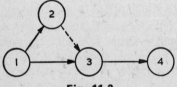

Fig. 11.3

practice, our activities (1–2) and (1–3) would be considerably elaborated.

Project Timing

We have seen how the network diagram indicates clearly
the relationship between activities, with regard to the
order in which they are to be performed. The diagram
can also be used to derive useful information regarding
the timing of the project.

For this purpose it is necessary to allocate a period of
time to each activity. This period is the minimum amount
of time in which the activity can reasonably be performed.
For routine types of work, the period can be accurately
estimated beforehand but for research projects, it is much
more difficult to determine it. It must also be remembered
that unforeseen difficulties can affect the rate of progress.

Any project planning technique must be able to take such difficulties in its stride.

Time can be measured in hours or days but weeks are usually used in project planning. For a normal five-day week, a day is then 0·2 of a week.

For any event in the network, the *earliest expected date* is the date upon which the event will occur if all preceding activities are completed within their specified times and if each activity is started as soon as preceding activities will allow. The earliest expected date for an event is calculated

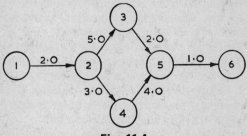

Fig. 11.4

by adding activity times along the longest (i.e., most time consuming) path from the network-beginning event to the event under consideration.

If we consider the particular case of the network-ending event, we obtain the earliest expected date for the completion of the project by adding activity times along the longest path through the network from beginning to end. This longest path is called the *critical path*. It is possible, of course, that there is more than one critical path. This is illustrated in Fig. 11.4 where activity times are shown. It will be seen that it takes 10 weeks to complete the project, this time being required by the two possible paths through the network. So both are critical paths.

For any event in the network, the *latest allowable date*

is the latest date upon which the event can occur without upsetting the scheduled completion date of the project. It is based on the assumption that all activities, after the event under consideration, will be completed within the times specified. To calculate the latest allowable date for an event, add together the activity times along the longest path between the event and the network-ending event. Then subtract the resulting amount of time from the scheduled completion date of the project.

For any event in the network, *slack time* is the difference between the latest allowable date and the earliest expected date. It follows from these definitions that along the critical path, all events have zero slack time.

By calculating the slack times for every event in the network, the planner can see clearly which activities must be kept up to date and which are comparatively unimportant. He may decide to switch men and resources from one part of the network to another in order to ensure that critical path activities are completed on time.

Referring again to our example of house building, let the figures on the right on page 158 be the activity times in weeks. Then the earliest expected date E, the latest allowable date L and the slack time S for each event in the network are given in the table on page 165. The critical path is

$$1\text{–}2\text{–}3\text{–}4\text{–}5\text{–}7\text{–}9\text{–}10$$

and we see that all these events have zero slack time. The remaining two events, 6 and 8, have a week slack time so these events can each fall a week behind schedule without affecting the completion date of the project.

Computer Application

When a network consists of very few activities, or when all its activities are personally known to and supervised by one manager, decisions concerning rearrangement and rescheduling can be quite simple. However, development of the more complex networks, specialization of managerial functions and an increase in the number of managerial echelons in a firm may lead to circumstances in which decisions must be based on secondhand data or information rather than on direct contact or personal observation.

When an organization becomes so large that persons making decisions in one part of the structure know little or nothing about what is going on in other parts of the structure, suboptimization may take place; that is, decisions may be made which the decision maker thinks are optimum when actually they serve to reduce the achievement of the total organization. As an example, a manager alters the arrangement of two activities in his part of the project to save a few hours of time; the result is to set back the master project three to four days.

	E	L	S
(1)	0	0	0
(2)	1·0	1·0	0
(3)	2·0	2·0	0
(4)	3·0	3·0	0
(5)	7·0	7·0	0
(6)	9·0	10·0	1·0
(7)	11·0	11·0	0
(8)	11·5	12·5	1·0
(9)	13·0	13·0	0
(10)	14·0	14·0	0

Another reason why computers are being put to work in the PERT process is their ability to generate masses of information quickly. In many companies there are some who receive operating statements as long as two months after the close of the operating periods to which they pertain. Reports concerning what a manufacturer's product cost last month may not be available until after that product is actually in the hands of the ultimate consumer. Moving closer to PERT, considerable expense can be the result of management's lack of up-to-date knowledge about certain parts of a project. For instance, if management learns early enough that the steelwork in a large building under construction is behind schedule, some arrangement might be worked out for the brick-layers who are to follow the steelworkers. If this falling behind in steelwork becomes known only a day or two before the bricklayers are to report for work, probably the only outcome will be higher labour costs than budgeted for in the project. In projects containing thousands of interconnected activities, information and data cannot be complete, accurate and current without the use of electronic computers.

The arithmetic of PERT calculations can be dealt with very quickly by a computer, though the computer program for PERT is difficult to write owing to the need to explore all the routes through the network. Once the program is written, however, it is available to the planner who needs only to specify the network and activity times in order to obtain the table on page 165. Having examined this table, the planner may decide to make adjustments. These adjustments can be fed into the computer to obtain a new table. And so the process can continue until the planner is satisfied that he has the best strategy.

Once the project gets under way, the network gradually melts away as events are achieved. However, due to unexpected delays, parts of the project will fall behind schedule and the planner may find that the critical path will alter. The need to reallocate resources is ever present until the entire project is complete. By means of a computer, the latest information about the progress of the project can be used at frequent intervals to revise the table of slack times.

Each of the activities which make up the network may be of a nature that can be dealt with by computer as was explained when we considered production control in Chapter 4.

Critical Path Method

The emergence of network techniques in the last decade has occurred due to the increasing need to keep projects within their specified time limits. This need in turn has arisen from the increasingly interwoven nature of industrial undertakings, many of which dwarf the greatest endeavours of previous ages. Indeed, the necessity to keep to time may be so great that considerable extra expense may be tolerated. It is to deal with such situations that the *critical path method* has been developed.

For this method, each activity in the network is given a normal time for completion and a *crash time* for completion. The crash time is shorter but can be achieved only at a higher cost. The cost of the activity must also be specified both for the normal and crash times. From these costs it is possible to calculate the cost per week of reducing the time of an activity. For example, suppose that for a particular activity, the normal time is 4 weeks at a cost of £1000 and the crash time is 2 weeks at a cost of £2000. Thus by 'crashing' the activity, 2 weeks can be saved but at an extra cost of £1000, i.e., £500 per week. This cost per week indicates which of the activities is cheapest to crash.

The problem which the method is intended to solve is this. Given a network with normal times for activities, it is desired to reduce the project time to a minimum. How can this minimum time be achieved with the least extra expense?

The method consists of selecting the activity on the critical path which is the cheapest to crash. This activity is then 'crashed' by writing in the crash time in place of the normal time. The next cheapest activity is then crashed and so on. During the course of this process, the critical path may change to a different route. The process is complete when all activities on the final critical path have been crashed. In arriving at this final network it may have been necessary to crash activities which do not lie on the final critical path. If so, each of these activities must be examined to see if it can be 'uncrashed' without disturbing the critical path. If so, then it is uncrashed. We then have the solution to the problem. The new cost of the project is obtained by adding the crash costs for crashed activities to the normal costs for the remaining activities.

Books by the author:

The Computer Handbook (Arthur Barker)
also available as
Computers (Pan)

Mathematics in Aeronautical Research (Oxford)

Your Book of Computers (Faber and Faber)
for children

Teach Yourself Analogue Computers (E.U.P.)

Computer Programming and Languages (Butterworths)

Index

Index

TEACH YOURSELF BOOKS

CYBERNETICS

F. H. George

This book is an introductory outline to the ramifications of the science we call 'Cybernetics'. As a science concerned with all matters of control and communication, it trespasses to some extent on what we have come to think of as the established sciences.

Teach Yourself Cybernetics covers both the pure theory of the science—mathematical, statistical and logical, and its application, which affects everything that human beings do especially how to learn, make decisions, plan, and solve problems, in such fields as Engineering, Management and Education. The author, Director of the Institute of Cybernetics at Brunel University, has been careful to write this general introduction in language intelligible to the layman.

'Professor George presents the thorough, educational and easily readable kind of book that one has come to expect of the *Teach Yourself* series.'

Times Literary Supplement

UNITED KINGDOM	40p
AUSTRALIA	$1.25*
NEW ZEALAND	$1.10

*recommended but not obligatory

ISBN 0 340 05941 9

TEACH YOURSELF BOOKS

ELECTRONIC COMPUTERS

F. L. Westwater

Electronic computers and computer technology are becoming increasingly part of our everyday lives. If there has been any technological revolution in the past few years, it has been in this field.

This book explains, with the help of illustrations, the use, principles and functions of digital computers. It is designed as a basic introduction to the complex subject of electronic computers and as such it will be of interest to those readers embarking on a career in computers, as well as to readers who come into contact with computers, either in business or through their many applications in everyday life, and who feel they want to learn more about computers.

Fully revised and updated, by an expert in the computer field, this book will be of interest to the specialist and interested layman alike.

UNITED KINGDOM	40p
AUSTRALIA	$1.25*
NEW ZEALAND	$1.10

*recommended but not obligatory

ISBN 0 340 09702 7

TEACH YOURSELF BOOKS

CRITICAL PATH ANALYSIS

D. W. Lang

This comprehensive introduction to the increasingly important field of Critical Path Analysis has been developed from experience in consultancy and teaching. It provides the basic knowledge necessary for the application of systematic reasoning to the planning and controlling of practical situations consisting of many separate, and often simultaneous, jobs. Illustrations, exercises and case studies enable the reader to apply the technique successfully and to appreciate the practical aspects of the subject.

UNITED KINGDOM	40p
AUSTRALIA	$1.25*
NEW ZEALAND	$1.10

*recommended but not obligatory

ISBN 0 340 11450 9

BUSINESS, PROFESSIONAL, COMPUTERS AND OFFICE PRACTICE BOOKS PUBLISHED BY *TEACH YOURSELF BOOKS*

BUSINESS, PROFESSIONAL, COMPUTERS AND OFFICE PRACTICE

16756 4	**Investment**	40p
	W.L.B. Fairweather	
12495 4	**Management Accounting**	50p
	B. Murphy	
12450 4	**Office Practice**	50p
	J. Shaw	
05975 3	**Operational Research**	60p
	M.S. Makower & E. Williamson	
11593 9	**O & M**	50p
	R.G. Breadmore	
05698 3	**Public Relations**	50p
	H. Lloyd	
05709 2	**Salesmanship**	40p
	S.A. Williams	
05712 2	**Secretarial Practice**	50p
	Pitmans College	
05687 8	**Shorthand**	40p
	Pitmans College	
18263 6	**Typewriting**	40p
	Pitmans College	

Available wherever *Teach Yourself Books* are sold.
For a complete list of *Teach Yourself Books* write to:

**St. Paul's House, Warwick Lane,
London EC4P 4AH.**

COMING SHORTLY:

Computer Programming/Fortran A.S. Radford

Computer Programming/Cobol   F.H. George